D0970305

ALSO BY JOAN RYAN

Little Girls in Pretty Boxes:
The Making and Breaking of Elite Gymnasts and Figure Skaters

WITH TARA VANDERVEER

Shooting from the Outside:
How a Coach and Her Olympic Team Transformed Women's Basketball

The Water Giver

The Story of a Mother,

a Son, and

Their Second Chance

JOAN RYAN

Simon & Schuster
New York   London   Toronto   Sydney

Simon & Schuster
1230 Avenue of the Americas
New York, NY 10020

First Simon & Schuster hardcover edition September 2009

SIMON & SCHUSTER and colophon are registered trademarks
of Simon & Schuster, Inc.

For information about special discounts for bulk purchases,
please contact Simon & Schuster Special Sales at
1-866-506-1949 or business@simonandschuster.com.

The Simon & Schuster Speakers Bureau can bring authors
to your live event. For more information or to book an event,
contact the Simon & Schuster Speakers Bureau at
866-248-3049 or visit our website at www.simonspeakers.com.

Designed by Nancy Singer

Manufactured in the United States of America

10 9 8 7 6 5 4 3 2 1

Library of Congress Cataloging-in-Publication Data
Ryan, Joan, date.
    The water giver / by Joan Ryan.
       p. cm.
    1. Motherhood—Psychological aspects. 2. Mothers and sons—California—
Anecdotes. 3. Ryan, Joan, date—Anecdotes. I. Title.
    HQ759.R93 2009
    155.6'463092—dc22
[B]   2009001533
ISBN: 978-1-4165-7652-5

To Ryan, my best teacher

The Water Giver

Prologue

I had not cried in his room. I believed he could hear me, or at least sense what I was feeling. So I chattered at him as if we were around our kitchen table. I told him we would be there when he woke up. That he should rest as long as he needed to heal. That he would be fine.

I believed it, despite everything that had happened. Ryan would be fine because children don't die and because he was Ryan. I looked at him on the bed in the intensive care unit and saw a strong, broad-shouldered, tanned sixteen-year-old who seemed to be sleeping. My eyes looked past the tube clamped to his mouth to keep him breathing, the hard plastic collar around his neck, the gauze turban, the wires snaking from his arms, chest, and skull into various beeping, blinking machines.

I stood at his bedside and held his hand and kissed his smooth skin. His fingernails still had grease under them from working at Lucky Garage. I wouldn't let the nurses clean them.

"You can't do this," I whispered in my son's ear. I was crying. "I can handle anything. But I can't handle losing you, Ryan. I can't survive that."

Part I

One

The bottom shelf of the bookcase in my home office is lined with black three-ring binders and manila folders marked "Ryan." They are filled with year-by-year educational plans, teacher conference notes, school transcripts, specialists' assessments, neuropsychiatrists' reports, photocopied articles about special-ed laws, positive discipline, learning disabilities, behavior modification techniques, attention deficit hyperactivity disorder.

They seem to chronicle a childhood. In truth they chronicle a motherhood.

The accumulation of information probably never helped Ryan very much. Oh, to some degree I'm sure it did. Mostly, though, the heaping piles of paper did for me what heaping piles of food do for others: they blunted my anxiety.

Ryan confounded me almost from birth. He was not the cooing cherub of my long-held imaginings, the come-to-life baby-doll I could dress up in soft sweaters and carry in the crook of my arm as I tested the temperature of his bottled milk on my wrist. Sometimes he was exactly that. Maybe often he was. The brain, I know, cannot be trusted with the past. It skips pages, whole chapters. It rewrites.

When I look back over Ryan's childhood, many of the good times are missing. What I have are fragments of the past, broken pieces that swirl behind my eyes late at night. I know even as I write this I am putting forth a picture that is incomplete and skewed.

In my memories, my baby is colicky and irritable. His mouth is open and his tongue recoiled and vibrating. I am in a T-shirt and sweats carrying him through the dark rooms of our house, bouncing him and singing and walking until finally I am crying, too, from exhaustion and the deflating realization that I have no clue how to comfort my own child.

In my memories, I have such poor mothering instincts that I watch the drunken wife of a second cousin teeter around a backyard barbecue with my two-month-old in her arms until my aunt shoots me a look, and when I do nothing, grabs the baby back. In my memories, four-year-old Ryan wanders from the house when I'm in the shower, and when I can't find him in the yard or on the sidewalk, I call the police and we find him crying at a neighbor's house. I don't immediately scoop him into my arms. I am afraid—because he is weird about being touched when he's upset—that he'll reject me in front of everybody. The neighbor lady, surely appalled, finally lurches forward and wraps her arms around him.

"I think this calls for hugs!" she says.

In my memories, when Ryan is nine, we are playing a pickup game of softball with my parents and siblings and aunts and uncles and cousins at a family reunion in New Jersey. Ryan hits a line drive to me in left field. He has never hit a ball as hard or as far. I catch it, much to the disbelief of the other adults. Wouldn't any other mother, knowing how important it is for this child to succeed in *something*, let the ball drop? It never occurs to me. Ryan runs off the field, angry and crying. Embarrassed, I run after him, past the disapproving faces in the row of lawn chairs by the backstop.

In my memories, Ryan is writhing and screaming from some minor provocation. As a toddler, he went nuts about shirt tags rubbing against his neck and about socks that weren't soft enough, ripping off clothes as if they were burning his skin. He screamed in the car when the sun made a direct hit on his eyes. When he was in preschool, I would wait by the phone for the teacher to tell me I had to come get him, that he had hit another child or exploded in another tantrum.

Sometimes I found myself so infuriated with Ryan—when he refused to stop banging his fork on his plate, or ripped toys from another child's hands, or shattered a neighbor's patio light by hitting golf balls from our yard into his, or butchered the bottoms of the kitchen cabinets yet again by skateboarding in the house— that I would come undone. It was as if his crackly irritability ricocheted around the room long after he left, so even in his absence it was often impossible to regroup. I screamed, usually at him, but sometimes into the air, a primal howl of exhaustion, frustration, fury. He alone had the ability to rip away my competent, she-has-it-figured-out outer self and expose the unhinged creature within, flailing to regain order and control.

Some of what Ryan and I did could seem funny in retrospect. When I told the stories, I would laugh, casting him as a Dennis-the-Menace character and me as the Looney-Tunes mom. But in the moment, as I marched him to the car after another meltdown at another birthday party, or when I lay awake at night, unable to let go of the day's events, I would feel angry at myself and this little boy for not being more than we were.

My husband, Barry, let much of Ryan's behavior slide off his back. He recognized our son's challenges and supported my efforts to find the right diagnoses and professional support. But he found ways to delight in Ryan. He loved Ryan's sense of humor, his affection for animals, his sweet way with babies and old people, his automatic but genuine "I love you" with every greeting and parting.

Barry looked at Ryan and saw what was wonderful about him. I looked at him and saw what needed fixing.

I attacked the puzzle of my son the way I attacked my stories as a journalist: by reading and studying, contacting experts, and compiling data. I went into full analytic mode. I seemed to believe that I could, with enough research and hard work, construct the child I wanted him to be. I became, over the years, less his loving mother and more his relentless reformer.

I was not the mother I imagined I would be. I was not the mother my son needed.

Then one horrible summer afternoon, I got a second chance.

Two

Ryan was born at 7:10 on a Thursday morning in June 1990 at Hemet Community Hospital near Palm Springs, California. Barry and I were asleep in a motel down the road. A twenty-year-old college student named Seyth had been in labor for more than twenty-four hours before delivering Ryan by C-section. We had met her over the phone four months earlier. We couldn't have children ourselves. During his first marriage, Barry had had a vasectomy after his second daughter was born, and a reversal was not likely to be successful. We had written a letter with our picture attached and given it to an adoption lawyer, who then distributed it around the country. Seyth had seen ours, along with a stack of others, at her doctor's office.

When she called us for the first time, she explained she was five months pregnant and living in Hawaii with her nineteen-year-old boyfriend, Tony. Both were born and raised on Oahu. Both wanted to finish college. They weren't ready for marriage, much less parenthood. It was too late for an abortion, though Seyth wasn't sure she would have considered one, anyway. She sounded bright and kind and practical. She told us she was the only child of divorced parents, who had died in the past year. Her father had been killed

when the backhoe he was driving flipped over; he had been putting the finishing touches on a home he had built in Maui. Seyth's
mother died of a brain aneurysm at her home in Idylwild, California, just weeks before Seyth called us. She and Tony were flying to
Idylwild to settle her estate. They said they would stay and have the
baby at the hospital in nearby Hemet.

When we hung up from that first call, Barry and I sat silent.

"What do you think?" he finally asked.

I said I liked them both a lot. Tony had gotten on the phone,
too, so we could get to know him a little. They sounded mature
and sure of what they wanted.

"But," I said, "how is she going to give up this baby after losing
both parents—her entire family—in the past year? She's had so
much loss already."

"I know."

Once she held the baby in her arms, I thought, she would
change her mind. But there was no reason to make a decision yet.
We had scheduled another phone call for the following week. We
would see. In the meantime, Seyth and Tony had sent a photo.
They were tanned and tall and smiling, arms around each other's
waists, leaning against a railing at what looked like a park.

Seyth's great-grandfather, we learned in the next call, had
been a Welsh doctor who joined an American Red Cross expedi-
tionary group to escape Russia during the revolution. They sailed
halfway around the world to Hawaii. He set up shop on Molokai,
the only doctor on the island, then moved to Oahu. The family
had been there ever since.

Tony came from a big Italian-Irish family. His father was an
executive with Traveler's Insurance and his mother a travel agent
who moved to Hawaii from the Midwest. Tony wanted to study
architecture in college. When Seyth's father died, Tony's family
took her in; they already had been dating for several years, since
the early days of high school. With the help of loose clothing, she
hid her pregnancy.

I thought they were terrific. I liked everything about them. Despite our doubts that Seyth would, in the end, be able to part with her baby, we decided to move forward. I took out their photo a million times over the next few months. I studied their faces: her olive skin and almond-shaped eyes, his wide forehead and square jaw. What would their baby—our baby—be? Barry and I bought a crib and a car seat but almost nothing else. I didn't want to face a home full of baby things if we returned from Hemet empty-handed.

When Tony called at dawn on June 27, 1990, to say Seyth had gone into labor, Barry and I hopped a flight to Ontario in Southern California, then drove into the 113-degree heat of Hemet. A dozen forest fires were sweeping across five thousand acres of Southern California, turning the sky in Hemet charcoal gray.

Folded neatly in our suitcase was a tiny yellow sunsuit and jacket.

We met Tony in the maternity ward waiting room. He was about six-feet-three-inches tall and broad-shouldered with dark eyes and an easy smile.

"Come meet Seyth," he said.

"Are you sure?" I asked.

"Definitely."

Seyth was propped against two pillows on a gurney in a small room, reading a magazine. She lit up when we walked in and shook our hands and asked if we had a pleasant trip. We said it was fine, thank you, how are you doing, unsure of what you are supposed to say to a woman about to give birth to your child. We asked if there was anything she needed and said that we would be right outside in the waiting room should she think of something.

Then she asked if we wanted to be in the delivery room when the baby arrived. "If it's all right with you," I said. "That would be wonderful."

We retreated to the waiting room, where Tony popped in and out, leaping up from the couch to check on Seyth, then bounding back to chat with us.

Around 2:00 A.M., Seyth still wasn't dilated enough to deliver. She would have to have a C-section. We couldn't be in the delivery room, after all. We drove the silent, stifling streets back to our motel and slept restlessly. We called the hospital at eight.

Seyth had delivered a boy. Eight pounds six ounces. Twenty inches long. In perfect health.

The baby was three hours old when we arrived at the nursery. Barry and I slipped on paper gowns, and I sat in a blue-cushioned rocking chair. A nurse placed the baby in my arms. Barry stood at my side, bending over to inspect this tiny creature. He had thick black hair that stuck up in every direction, perfect little fingers, huge dark eyes that opened and closed as if in slow motion.

All the walls we had erected to protect ourselves crumbled quickly and quietly. I fed the baby a bottle, watching his cheeks rise and fall, studying his little fingernails, and breathing in his sweet baby smell. Then Barry held him as the nurse stripped him for a diaper change. Ryan pooped in Barry's hand, a story that, later, never failed to send Ryan into spasms of laughter.

During the course of the day, I visited Seyth twice in her room. She was in pain from the cesarean section, but she was cheerful. She had held and even breast-fed the baby. I knew this because when I left Seyth's room, a nurse made it a point to tell me. "She's not giving him up *now*," she said, waving her hand as if dismissing any hope we had of taking the baby home.

During my second visit to Seyth's room, she said she and Tony had a request.

"We have nothing to give our baby, so we'd like to give him a middle name," she said. They had chosen Iokepa, Hawaiian for Joseph, Tony's middle name.

We had planned to name the baby David Ryan Tompkins: Barry's middle name, my last name, and Barry's last name. Instead we named him Ryan Iokepa Tompkins. Seyth and Tony signed the release papers. They still had six months to change their minds, but they were so clear about their decision that Barry and

I weren't worried. (Six months later, in the chambers of a Marin County judge, the adoption became final.)

When the doctor cleared Ryan to leave the hospital, he was thirty hours old.

Seyth helped me dress him in the yellow sunsuit and jacket. She held him while I slipped his tiny arms into the sleeves. My throat burned from the tears I held back, knowing if I let go, I would crumple into a quivering heap.

Then in the single most courageous act I have ever witnessed, Seyth handed me her baby.

"I'm happy you're going to be his parents," she said. "I'm really happy you're going to make a nice home for him."

She cried and I cried. Barry, overwhelmed, had already left to get the car. I can't remember if Tony was in the room or not.

We drove out of Hemet, the skies still dark with smoke. I sat in the back of the rental car, next to Ryan's car seat, and stared at him. He stared back. He had a perfect little face. Of all the babies in the world, this one had landed in our backseat. This eight pounds, six ounces of squishy fat and downy skin was my son. I repeated it in my head, as if to convince myself it finally was true.

My son. My son. My son.

Ryan at two weeks old, asleep in my arms.

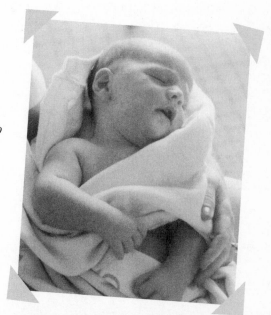

Three

I set out to raise Ryan the way I was raised. My son would listen to his parents. He would do his homework. He would do his chores. He would fall into line. My parents managed to get six children to sit quietly at mass and clean their rooms and finish their peas. How hard could it be to tame one?

But straight-out discipline didn't work. As a toddler and pre-schooler, Ryan didn't seem to respond to consequences. Or rather, he responded in the moment—he cried about being banished to his room or banned from watching TV, for example—but time-outs didn't keep him from repeating the same behavior again and again. Nothing stopped the tantrums. Nothing stopped the irritability, the lashing out, the aggression with other children, the defiance that triggered my own furious tantrums.

But for as much as Ryan drove me out of my mind, I loved him with a fierceness that could make me cry just to look at him sometimes. And he loved me. No matter what sharp words passed between us during the day, at night we could sink into each other and just be mother and son. I would read to him, the two of us sitting in bed under the covers. Then I would sing "American Pie" or some other 1970s songs I knew by heart and stroke his hair. Sometimes, as a toddler, he talked about our trips to Hawaii, which he loved from his first visit when he was just a year old, as if he knew these were his roots. He was an island boy, at home in the ocean. When he got older, he slipped through the waves like a fish, as if the water were as elemental to him as air.

Sometimes Ryan mused about God. When he was four years old, he wondered aloud if only God was real and we were just his dream. He once told me that inside each person are boxes inside boxes, hundreds of thousands of them. You could open one each day until you were twenty, then one each year. At the center, he said, is perfection. Some people get so far as to cut the tape off the final box. He informed me that I had 103 more boxes. I said I'd be dead before I got to the perfect one. He said I'd open it in heaven with God.

When Ryan and I finished our talks at night and his eyes grew heavy, we would tell each other, "I love you more than all the stars in the sky," or all the sand on the beach, all the hubcaps on all the cars in the world, all the chocolate chips in all the cookies ever baked—the sayings became sillier as the years went on.

Ryan at ten months old on his first trip to Hawaii.

"You're the best kid in the world," I would say when I turned out the light.

"You're the best mom in the world."

"I love you, baby-babe."

"I love you, too, Mommy-mom."

But the quiet magic of bedtime too often disappeared with the morning alarm.

Four

One autumn day, when Ryan was four, he was riding his tricycle around the table on our back deck. We were eating lunch with Barry's parents, who were then in their late seventies.

Barry's mother, Rose, left to retrieve something from the house. She didn't see the screen across the doorway and stepped into it. She bounced off and tumbled backward down two steps. She lay on the deck stunned though not injured.

Ryan freaked. He kicked his tricycle over. He yelled. He knocked over a chair. He stomped around, punching at Barry and me as we tried to calm him. He was agitated for at least thirty minutes, long after Barry's mother had gotten up and assured him she was fine.

We began to realize that what seemed at first to be isolated tantrums—reacting violently to the smell of smoke and the car heater, the feel of certain fabrics, the presence of dust, the temperature of food, the pitch and volume of people's voices—were in fact almost everyday behaviors. Ryan would throw himself on the floor or flail at us or his preschool teachers, landing his share of whacks and punches. He was clumsier and less coordinated than most kids his age. He couldn't jump, for example, and he looked like a bag of spare parts when he ran. He also seemed to be hyperaware of kids bumping into him and almost oblivious when he bumped into and even knocked down other children.

What was wrong with this kid? And how do we fix him? I went into research mode. I had come to believe through my career in journalism that diligence and smarts could solve any problem. I convinced myself I could learn to navigate even the most unfamiliar terrain because I had done it before, in particular when I became a sportswriter.

I was an unlikely pioneer. I was a behind-the-scenes person—so shy as a kid my face flushed and my heart pounded at the mere *thought* of raising my hand in class. I majored in journalism but took the editing track, satisfied to correct other people's stories and write headlines, figuring this would someday lead to a spot on the masthead. I was introverted, yes, but not without ambition.

A few months into my first job at the *Orlando Sentinel* in 1982, I concluded that I would never climb the newspaper ladder without putting in at least a little time as a reporter. All the top editors had been reporters at some point. I had always admired the writing in the sports section. I had grown up in a sporty family—my father had cared more about my softball batting average than my grade-point average.

I mentioned to a colleague on the copy desk that at some point I might like to write sports. Before I knew it, word had reached the editor-in-chief, and in the summer of 1983, I was working on the copy desk in the *Sentinel* sports department, the first woman to cross that threshold.

I soon found myself hanging out most nights after the final edition with the wonderful motley crew of sports guys: the sweet forty-five-year-old Alfred E. Newman look-alike who still lived with his mother; the quiet divorced copy editor who piped up with answers to our most obscure fact-checking questions; the twenty-something clerk who, with a wink, introduced himself to me as Well-Hung McClung; a gorgeous dark-haired married football writer who pretended not to notice my stammering and flushing when I spoke with him; and Bill, the lanky, funny, gregarious ringleader of the copy desk who answered my stupidest questions without making me feel like an idiot.

I started drinking scotch, learning early on never to order a drink "the color of baby clothes," as one editor put it. I became adept at using fuck in all its grammatical applications. I ditched my father's Nova and bought a 1979 Trans-Am with a 405 engine. I was having a blast. The sports editor began interspersing my copy-editing shifts with assignments to cover a tennis match here and a minor league baseball game there. I would get almost sick with fright before each assignment.

One day I was covering a yacht race in Tampa. I was in the press tent, typing on a portable computer that weighed nearly as much as I did. (To send the story, we had to shove the phone's handset into two rubber cups, enter a phone number into the computer, listen for the high-pitched tone, and press *Send*. We usually repeated the process three or four times before the story actually went through, a frustrating ordeal on deadline that led to many telephone handsets smashing against many press-box desks.)

"The masts sliced the air like stilettos," I began, composing a story that prompted the paper's managing editor to pop his head into the sports department the next day.

"Beautiful story," he said.

I felt for the rest of the day as if I had won the lottery, repeating the compliment in my head in order to relive the flush of pleasure.

Not long afterward, I was asked to fill in as a columnist when one of the regulars went on vacation. I wrote what I thought was a humorous essay on why golf is not a sport. When I turned it in, my friends on the copy desk looked at me as if I had lost my mind.

"You don't want to do this," one said.

"What do you mean?"

The editor of the paper had two sacred loves in his life: the San Francisco 49ers and golf.

"It's just poking a little fun," I said. I couldn't imagine the editor could take golf so seriously that he would be offended by a little ribbing about lime-green polyester pants and beer bellies.

Early the next morning, the day the column ran, my roommate hollered from the kitchen that my editor was on the phone. My heart stopped. Shit. What had I been thinking?

"I read your column," he said.

I could barely breathe.

"I'm giving you a $50-a-week raise," he said. "It took balls to write that."

I was starting to warm to sportswriting.

Then I entered my first locker room.

I had been sent to a U.S. Football League game between the Orlando Renegades and the Birmingham Stallions. It was 1984. By then, I had almost a year under my belt of covering the University of Central Florida football and basketball teams. The college players had always come out of the locker room after games to talk to me.

But at halftime that March night in Orlando, the snippy PR guy for the Stallions said no, he couldn't bring players out of the locker room. If I wanted to interview running back Joe Cribbs—the focus of my story—I would have to go in.

As the game clock counted off the final seconds, my stomach churned. I rode the elevator to the bowels of the stadium and, as luck would have it, arrived at the Stallions locker room before any other reporters. I looked at the door. I looked at my watch. I had about an hour before deadline. That meant about fifteen minutes to interview Cribbs, five minutes to race back down the hall and up the elevator to the press box, and forty minutes to write and send my story.

I felt the familiar pounding of my heart in my ears. I pushed the door and took two steps inside. It smelled like mold and thrummed with shouts and laughs and running water. Massive men in various stages of undress, some naked, walked across my path, traveling between the lockers on the right and the showers on the left. I scanned the room for Cribbs, then suddenly stopped, mortified that the players might think I was checking them out. I dropped my eyes to the notebook clutched in my damp hand. Now how do I find Cribbs without actually looking?

As panic set in, the room suddenly fell silent. I looked up. A hundred eyes took me in, gaping as if a three-headed Martian had just materialized in their midst. Then they erupted, roaring obscenities and crude jokes. They were outraged, indignant, and having the time of their lives.

"Where is Joe Cribbs's locker?" I stammered.

On a bench next to me sat an enormous shirtless player cutting tape off his ankle with a long-handled razor.

"Can you tell me where Joe Cribbs's locker is?" I repeated, directing the question to the seated player. He didn't look up.

Suddenly I felt something slide up my calf toward the hem of my skirt.

The player on the bench was running the long handle of the razor up my leg.

"*What* are you doing?" I yelled, yanking my leg away.

Humiliated and furious, I wheeled around. In the doorway stood a middle-aged man in a red V-neck sweater, the kind I had noticed on all the Stallions' coaches. He was smiling in a way that made me want to punch him in the face, if I had been that sort of person. I brushed past him and out of the locker room.

"Look," I said, turning back toward him, trying to modulate my voice. "I'm trying to do my job here. This isn't okay."

The V-neck sweater guy smiled wider.

"You're entering on your own initiative, so you're subject to what goes on in there," he said. "It is not a proper place for a female to be."

He was defending these guys? This was *my* fault? Before I could explode, I caught sight of the PR guy and grabbed his arm.

"I need to talk to Joe Cribbs," I said. "You have to bring him out here."

He headed toward the locker room. Five minutes slipped by. Ten. I'd have thirty minutes to write. Finally, Cribbs emerged. I asked him a few bad questions, he gave me a few bad answers, then I sprinted back up to the press box and wrote a few bad paragraphs. But I made deadline.

In flipping through the Stallions' media guide later the next day, I recognized the man in the V-neck sweater as the team president.

Christ. It's one thing for the players to act like bullies. But the team president? He believed, as the players did, that I had no business covering that game, much less entering the sanctuary of the locker room. When my sports editor asked me to write a column about the experience, readers rallied behind the players. They depicted me in their letters as everything from a whore to a voyeur.

The backlash was a revelation.

The players, coaches, owners, and fans really, really didn't want me to do this job.

Suddenly I really, really wanted to be a sportswriter.

The episode in the locker room tapped into something elemental, something I had not felt since my softball days—specifically, the crystalline moment of digging into the batter's box against a pitcher and deciding she was not going to beat me.

Soon after the Stallions' episode, my editor/mentor was hired as the editor at the *San Francisco Examiner*, and he hired me as a full-time sports columnist, one of the first women in the country to hold that position. I learned to ignore the jockstraps that occasionally pelted my back inside the locker rooms and the players who disrobed the moment I approached their lockers. Because the locker room was the official interviewing area—a fact overlooked by most fans and even players—I couldn't do my job without going in.

I was in the 49ers locker room after a game in 1985, my first year in San Francisco, when a well-dressed man tapped me on the shoulder. He asked if I was Joan Ryan, a pretty good guess considering I was the only woman in the locker room. He introduced himself as Barry Tompkins, a friend of the *Examiner* editor who had brought me out from Orlando. He was a sportscaster for HBO. I was polite but basically blew him off. I was on deadline. I had no time to chat.

Eight months later, I was having lunch with another local sports columnist at the Washington Square Bar & Grill, a popular hangout for newsies. Barry was at the next table with a friend. I had only a vague recollection of meeting him in the locker room. But he knew my colleague, and the four of us ended up talking through lunch. I liked how easily he laughed and how he treated the busboy with as much respect as the restaurant's owner, who had come by to greet him. He was handsome and well spoken and worldly. I figured I didn't have a chance.

I found out later that Barry had called his friend Stephanie, who worked with me at the *Examiner*, after lunch.

"Tell me about Joan Ryan," Barry said. "I have a rule about not dating anyone under thirty." I was twenty-six. Barry was forty-five.

"Break your rule," Stephanie said.

Three days later, Barry called from New York and left a message on my answering machine, asking if I would have dinner with him when he returned home later that week. He took me to a beautiful restaurant, but I was so nervous that I pushed the lobster ravioli around my plate, unable to swallow a bite. My face radiated from a sunburn I had gotten that afternoon at Baker Beach. I wore a dowdy pink-print pleated skirt and an oversized black leather jacket. I still marvel that he asked me out on a second date.

I was smitten, setting aside all the factors going against us. He was older, Jewish, an only child. I was young, Catholic, from a large family. He was a fashion plate, flying to Montreal to have his suits tailor-made. I wore Levi's and had yet to discover heels or eyeliner. He knew wine and how to order in French and what to tip the bellman at the Four Seasons. I knew Birds-Eye, Mrs. Paul's, and Grand Slam breakfasts at Denny's.

He had been married for ten years and had lived with a girl-friend for seven. My personal record in a sustained relationship was six months. He had two grown children and no desire for more. He wanted to hop planes to Paris and eat dinner at ten and have white sofas in the living room. I wanted to make Halloween costumes and read *Green Eggs and Ham* and tape finger-paint art to my refrigerator.

We were an unlikely couple.

Yet about a year after we began dating, I asked Barry to marry me, and he said yes. Then I said the offer came with a condition: we had to have at least one child. He said okay.

Barry and I were constantly flying off in different directions to our various sporting events, talking daily by phone, and return-ing to San Francisco with stories and gossip. In his career, Barry had covered just about every major sports event in the world. I was a rookie, still a little stunned to find myself at the Olympics or World Series, the Super Bowl or Wimbledon, sitting elbow to elbow with Dave Anderson of the *New York Times* and Jim Mur-ray of the *LA Times*. I learned how to convince myself—at least for the time it took to write my piece—that I was as good as they were. I pretended to *be* them. Eventually, by listening and watch-ing, I developed my own style and quietly built respect for what I produced.

My success in sports and my role as a pioneer surprised even my family, perhaps especially my family. Though always a compet-itive student and athlete, I was so quiet and unremarkable among my five brothers and sisters that when a friend asked my mother a few years ago to tell her about my childhood, she couldn't think of a single story.

In time, writing sports turned me into someone who felt self-assured, even bulletproof. It was as if having survived—and triumphed over—the people who hoped to drive me away, nothing could rattle me. I could talk to anyone. Most miraculous of all, through the guidance of a speaking coach, I learned how to speak in public, finally building up the confidence to accept speaking engagements and appear on television.

I believed I could handle anything.

Then I became a mother.

Five

After the freak-out over Barry's mother's fall, Ryan saw his first specialist and received his first diagnosis.

A top psychologist and occupational therapist at California Pacific Medical Center in San Francisco said Ryan had sensory integration dysfunction. It is most common among children with autism, though Ryan was not autistic. Ryan's diagnosis meant he had an underdeveloped central nervous system. It did a poor job of processing the information he received through his senses. He had an oversensitivity to touch, particularly when he was agitated, yet he also needed things in his hands at all times, seeming to crave the stimulation of certain objects. He was overly sensitive to tiny details in his environment, unable to ignore a fly outside the window or the drip of a faucet, yet he completely missed obvious visual cues like body language. He was overly sensitive to noise, yet he couldn't discern tone of voice and often missed the actual meaning of what people said.

We were told that children with sensory integration dysfunction overreact to life's stresses and demands. They also have problems with motor planning, the sequence of muscle functions

necessary to form letters or ride a bike. They have difficulty stopping one activity and moving on to something else. They get
stuck. They can be inflexible and irrational, unable to see another point of view.

For six months, we drove Ryan into San Francisco twice a
week for occupational therapy. The OT taught us techniques we
could use at home to help him learn to monitor, modulate, and
respond to stimuli. We brushed him with a soft brush, ran a rolling
pin over his back and limbs, got him to jump into pillows and bur-
row under blankets, engaged him in controlled roughhousing.

He was better but only by degree. I was more patient with him.
There was a diagnosis, which meant his behavior wasn't completely his fault. And it meant it wasn't completely mine, either.
Kindergarten was about to start. I had mixed feelings. On the one
hand, I was excited for Ryan, and I was hopeful the therapies had
taken care of the worst of his behaviors. On the other hand, I felt
a vague dread. At home, Barry and I could protect him. We and
his grandparents and his babysitters loved him, whines and temper tantrums and all, because he was such a sweet, affectionate kid
and because such love is unconditional.

Beyond our gate, there would be conditions, and Ryan could
not possibly meet all of them. No schoolchild ever has. He would
not wear the right clothes one day. Or he would be slow in learning multiplication. At school, along with his numbers and letters,
he would learn failure, humiliation, betrayal, loneliness. They
were part of growing up; I knew that. Ryan had no idea.

On his first day of kindergarten, Ryan arrived at the side of my
bed with his socks in one hand, a Lego contraption in the other,
and a green T-shirt clamped between his teeth. He dropped the
shirt on my bed.

"Mom," he whispered. "Is this the school day?"

"It sure is."

"Good!" he said, as if he were setting sail for Alaska.

He had this vision, I think, of suddenly sprouting into adulthood as he passed through the classroom door. He seemed to think kindergarten held the answers to all the great mysteries of the grown-up world—writing and reading, tying shoelaces, riding a two-wheeler, using knives, driving. I half expected him to examine his chin in the bathroom mirror for stubble.

In the kitchen, he climbed atop a chair and a thick pillow and ate his Cheerios.

"Mom, it's Josephine's birthday today." He smiled.

This was a running joke. It was always Josephine's birthday.

Josephine was an imaginary black cat who lived with us. She was a useful cat. Whenever someone in the family burped or made a spill, one of us cried, "Josephine!" Ryan announced her birthday every four or five days so we had an excuse to make a cake or buy cupcakes and Ryan could blow out the candles.

Ryan also had imaginary brothers. They were all named Sam. There was plain Sam (the original brother) and Michael Sam, Stephen Sam, and so on. They rode motorcycles and carried guns and flew airplanes and built houses. They had been everyplace and done everything, which is what Ryan wanted for himself and what kindergarten seemed to promise.

I parked the car at the side of the school. Even at 8:20, it was so hot the marigolds along the curb were shriveling up on their stems. Ryan jumped over the cracks in the sidewalk. A dense pack of mothers and fathers, some with video cameras, had gathered outside the front door. The two kindergarten teachers handed out nametags.

"I can do it," Ryan said. His thick fingers fiddled with the safety pin. Then: "Mom, you can do it."

We went inside to a large, clean classroom with walls lined with cubbies and shelves of crayons and construction paper. On the counters were three computers and a microwave oven and, on the floor, a gray rabbit named Shadow. The children sat around the teacher, Mrs. McDonald, who soon asked the parents to leave. I gave Ryan a hug and started out.

"Mom!" He ran after me. "When are you picking me up?"

"At lunchtime. Have a great day."

I fought back tears. Ryan was starting on a wonderful adventure, yet it felt more like an ending to me. I could almost feel his fingers slipping from my hand.

Soon Ryan forgot about the Sams and Josephine. His made-up world gave way to test scores and homework and social expectations.

School did not play to Ryan's strengths: his imagination, his big heart, his energy. By third grade, school became almost torturous for him—and us. He couldn't sit still. He couldn't write cursive letters or perform simple math, much less memorize his multiplication tables. In conversation, he'd fall silent for long moments as he tried to retrieve a word. His brain, I explained to him, was like a dry-cleaner's rack. All his words were hanging on the rack like clothes, and when he pushed the button to bring them around to the front, sometimes they were close by and sometimes they were all the way in the back. A conversation with Ryan could be exhausting. He could not deliver a coherent account of, say, a field trip to a museum, the tale starting in the middle, doubling back to the beginning, then jumping to a 1969 Camaro he saw in the parking lot, then concluding with the inevitable question, "What did you ask me?"

But sometimes his sensitivity could stop me in my tracks.

When Ryan was seven years old, he was helping me clean out a closet. I left to answer the phone. When I returned, Ryan was crying. He was sitting cross-legged on the floor, and on his lap was what we called his adoption book. It was an album filled with the letters of recommendation from friends, legal documents, scribbled notes from phone conversations, congratulatory cards—and a photo of Tony and Seyth, Ryan's birth parents. He knew their names and the circumstances of his birth. He had never known what they looked like.

"Sweetie, what is it?" I asked, sitting down next to him and rubbing his back. He didn't want to tell me.

"It will hurt your feelings," he said.

I told him that he would not hurt my feelings.

"They don't know me," he said, his voice catching on his sobs.

"You can miss people you've never met," I said. "They're a part of you."

I led him to bed and crawled in next to him, taking him in my arms. I assured him that we would visit Hawaii when he was older and he could meet them. He cried until he fell asleep.

These were the times I wondered how I could be so hard on him. There was such a sweetness about him.

During his years in Little League—when I coached, playing out my own Norman Rockwell fantasies—Ryan was more likely to be petting a dog in the outfield than chasing a fly ball. He once jogged into the dugout from right field, pulled a lizard from his back pocket, and spent most of the remaining innings transforming a helmet cubby into a comfortable habitat of grass and twigs.

Ryan doted on Barry's mother until the day she died at the age of eighty-four. He would listen for hours to the stories of the elderly residents at her assisted living center, pressing for more details about what it was like during the Depression or World War II. He treasured his grandfather's old drafting tools: mechanical pencils and slide rules and compasses.

He seemed to love everything old, things with a history and a story, so whenever I wanted to get him out of the house, all I had to do was suggest a trip to the antique stores in Petaluma. He loved antiques for their stories, their uniqueness. He seemed to recognize that if an item was one of a kind, it was valuable. I

have wondered if part of the attraction was also the flaws and dis-
placed quality of antiques. They existed out of time, looking for a
place to land. Ryan scoured garage sales and the huge metal debris
boxes people parked outside their houses during spring cleanups.
He would return home with some chipped, bent, or dented dis-
card, as if he were rescuing it and putting it back to work, recognizing a value in it that others didn't.

His interest in old things bordered on the obsessive; I had to
drag him out of garage sales and antique stores when, after waiting for him to look at every single piece, I was ready to faint from
boredom.

I told myself I should be meeting his eruptions and bad behavior with compassion and love instead of anger and judgment.
But I couldn't. My motherhood was still more about me. I was still
raising the child I expected, not the child I had.

I continued to be embarrassed by every call from the school or
from another parent reporting on Ryan's misbehavior. I couldn't
always hide from Ryan my resentment at the position he was putting me in, which, intellectually, I knew was a horrible thing to
lay on a kid. Still, there it was, this ugly, petty, selfish response—
which, of course, only deepened my conviction that I was an in-
competent mother. Instead of helping my child, I was feeding the
storms roiling inside him.

"I'm reading *Portnoy's Complaint*," I wrote in a journal when
Ryan was eight years old. We were in Bangkok on a three-day
stopover before going on to Bali for vacation. Ryan had been
whiny and irritable on the flight, behaving like a spoiled brat. I
had responded by getting angrier and angrier. Now I was awake at
4:15 A.M., sitting in the bathroom of our hotel room.

"I'm thinking about me as the critical, castrating mother (in
the novel)," I wrote. "I feel I am like that with Ryan, that I'm
conveying to him that he'll never be good enough, that he is pe-
rennially a disappointment. I am at a loss about how to be a good
mother. I truly can't say if I'm too hard on him or too soft."

Homework that took other kids thirty minutes took Ryan two hours. He would sharpen his pencil sixteen times until it was the size of a paper clip, and then, claiming it was too small to hold, start over on another pencil. Later, in fifth grade, he began a habit of filling in all the closed circles in the letters of his homework sheet, unable to stop himself until the page looked like it had contracted measles. Before even reading the directions of an assignment, he would convince himself that he didn't understand what was being asked of him.

He struggled in particular with time. We always joked that only two times existed for Ryan: now and not now. He couldn't tell time on a traditional clock or name the months of the year in order. When we returned from a summer trip to Africa when he was ten, he asked if we had missed Christmas.

Even when he began middle school, he rarely knew, at any moment, the time, the month, or the day of the week, despite the calendars and clocks we had hung all over the house. He never knew what time his classes began or ended; he followed classmates who had the same schedule as he did. The digital watches we strapped to his wrist seemed to disappear as quickly as we bought them.

Most distressing, he was still exploding. He threw a coffee mug against my bedroom wall. He pushed over a desk in class. He tore up his homework over the slightest frustration. Ryan almost always felt guilty and embarrassed afterward. He'd say he hated himself for being so stupid and getting so angry. And the next day we were likely to have a wonderful time and he would be the greatest kid in the world.

The basics of child rearing that worked perfectly well for my five siblings and me had little effect on Ryan. Not that Barry and I executed this discipline the same way my parents did. They lived three thousand miles away, but I could hear their voices in my head: all that kid needs is a good whack.

Six

Whacking didn't come as naturally to me as it did to my parents, even though I weathered my share of flat-handed slaps and belts across the rear as a kid. My three brothers got it worse than my two sisters and me. My father was soft on us girls, relatively speaking. But when the simmering rage bubbled over and we saw the gritted teeth, the jutted jaw, the vein in his scarlet neck pop like a rope, we knew one or more of the boys was about to get it.

His anger, so sudden and unpredictable, both scared and angered me. He sometimes pulled into the driveway from work and started yelling before he reached the front door. Maybe we had left our bikes out or had not cut the grass. It seemed almost anything could set him off, and whatever fun thing we had been doing— baking cookies, playing Monopoly—would be ruined.

My father grew up in the Bronx, one of eight children to second-generation Irish immigrants. They had nothing. His father was a charming cabbie who drank too much, pummeled his boys just for looking at him funny, and gave the shirt off his back to anyone who needed it. He died when my father was a child, and his widow, destitute, fed her brood by standing in line every week for government-issue cheese, oatmeal, and margarine. My mother recalls visiting my father's family for the first time when they were dating and watching roaches crawl over the phone and up the wall. My grandmother's second husband was a drunk who couldn't keep a job.

My father was accepted to then-prestigious Bedford Stuyvesant High School but dropped out in the ninth grade. He didn't like going to class, and his mother needed help with the bills. He took a job working the graveyard shift as a janitor in a downtown office building, then joined the army during the Korean War. The war ended soon after he arrived. My brothers and sisters and I believed his story (long after we should have) that the North Koreans promptly surrendered when they heard he was coming. That's how formidable he seemed to us.

I thought my father's rough upbringing explained the darkness that often roiled inside his head. Only later did I discover that I didn't know the whole story.

My mother grew up in a more middle-class neighborhood of the Bronx, also with Irish Catholic parents. Her father was a welder and her mother a phone operator at Con-Ed. She was the middle of three girls. Two additional sisters died: one in infancy, the other as a toddler. My sister Barbara carries the name of one and I of the other. My mother married at twenty-one and had six children before she was thirty. I have no memories of her eating, only smoking Parliaments and drinking Tetley tea. She was the one we could talk to, who would listen to our long, rambling stories about some incident at school or the plot of some book we had borrowed from the library.

But, like my father, she had her moments. We would come home from school some afternoons to find our clothes strewn across the side lawn. She had tossed them from our second-floor bedrooms, fed up with the mess. She once rampaged through the house after my brother Bobby took a permanent black marker to the Formica she had just spent five hours cutting and gluing to the kitchen counter. She yanked books off shelves, knocked clothes from their hangers, and screamed at a feral-like pitch I came to recognize and understand only when I became a mother myself.

Our family was like most families we knew; everyone yelled and whacked their kids. We were a close family. We were, in spite of everything, happy. My mother put on little summer parties for the six of us in the backyard with our inflatable wading pool. She taught us how to make perfume from water and rose petals. She and my father hosed down the yard in the winter to create a skating rink. When we lived in New Jersey, my parents took us every October to Tice's Farm to choose a pumpkin and drink apple cider and eat cinnamon donuts crisp and warm from the deep fryer. Every summer on August 3, my brother Kenneth's birthday, we rode the roller coasters and ate cotton candy at Palisades Amusement Park.

On Sundays, the six of us kids, cleaned and combed, attended mass, filing like a small army through the massive front doors. We stopped in the vestibule, one at a time, to dip our fingers into the

On our way to Easter mass in front of our New Jersey house in 1966. Back row, left to right: me, Bobby, Barbara. Front row, left to right, Gerard, Donna, Kenneth.

bowl of holy water and touch our forehead, chest, and shoulders in the sign of the cross. The water looked no different from what poured from our kitchen tap, but I had seen the priest sprinkle it over the heads of babies at the baptismal font. My parents said the water cleansed the baby of original sin. With just a few drops, the baby was more or less reborn with an absolutely clean slate. I didn't know what was in the water, but I knew it held some sort of magic that kept us safe. Sometimes I dipped twice.

On summer weekends, there always seemed to be a communion or an anniversary or a birthday, and we'd have a yard filled with relatives drinking Pabst Blue Ribbon beer from glass mugs, listening to the Yankees game on the transistor radio, and ducking the Wiffle balls we sent careening past their heads. When it got dark, we caught fireflies and played flashlight tag, said our prayers, and went to bed: the three girls in one room, the three boys in another. My father would go from bed to bed tickling each of us until, breathless and pained from laughter, we begged him to stop.

Barbara, Donna, and Kenneth still live within a mile of my parents in southern Florida. Gerard lives two-and-a-half hours north in a suburb of Orlando. Bobby's story, I will tell later. Barbara, Donna, and Ken and their children get together almost every Sunday on my parents' back patio, screened in to keep the mosquitoes out and let the warm Florida air in. They drink wine and beer and tell stories and laugh and skewer each other with brutal humor; we are a survival-of-the-fittest kind of family. After dinner, my father will ask who wants Irish coffee and pour the Tullamore Dew into Irish coffee glasses, a full shot each, and shake the cream so it sits like a thick cloud atop the coffee and whiskey.

I loved visiting from California, even though my parents had long since moved from the house where I last had a bed of my own. Their new house had none of the smells I recognized. I didn't know where to find the salad bowl or extra bed linens. But I would settle into a cushioned patio chair and sink right back into the familiar banter and rhythm of my childhood.

Or at least I could when I didn't bring Ryan.

When Ryan came with me, my stomach twisted in knots. The other grandchildren, having grown up around my parents, knew the house rules (no walking around with a can of soda, for instance; no food outside the dining room). They jumped when my mother or father barked at them. Ryan was oblivious to the rules or to my parents' irritated tone of voice. I knew he would misbehave, that he would come across as an undisciplined kid whose mother couldn't control him. My anxiety surely fed Ryan's impulsivity and distractibility, making matters worse. The visits were usually disappointing, if not quite disastrous, and I always left feeling like a failure.

I would start believing, once again, that Ryan's real problem was that we were just too easy on him. He was an only child. He was growing up in an affluent community. He felt entitled. He was spoiled. Or maybe it really was me. I wasn't patient and understanding enough. I wasn't the kind of mother a child like him needed.

I didn't know what to believe.

Those were my pinball years, when I ricocheted between thinking Ryan's problems would be solved with the right diagnosis and treatment, then thinking—with equal conviction—that they would be solved by just cracking the whip and knocking him into next week.

When I waited for Ryan at the end of the school day, I would study the *Good Mothers*. They were amazing, marvelous, right out of a magazine. They brought cupcakes when they were assigned to bring cupcakes. They remembered gifts for the teachers on Valentine's Day and Christmas, always wrapped in color-coordinated paper and ribbon. They exercised regularly while the kids were at school. They had left successful careers to devote themselves to motherhood. They were patient and kind. Around them I felt the way I did in press boxes early in my career: I was out of my league, unable to grasp how to be as good as they were.

I'd go home and read another book on learning disabilities or behavior plans, even though as time passed I became less confident that research and intellect would make me a better mother. I was like someone trying to learn how to dance from a manual, counting steps in her head, utterly incapable of surrendering herself to the music.

Seven

My friend Chris was one of the good mothers. She had been an executive at Bank of America before she and her husband, Eric, adopted twin baby girls, and for a few years, they cared for the girls' older brother while his birth mother was having problems. Chris had waited so long to become a mother and threw herself into the job as if born to it. When the girls started school, Chris and Eric adopted a third child, a three-year-old boy named Scott.

Chris loved having a house full of children, and when we moved in three doors down, Ryan soon became an unofficial member of her brood. He was four-and-a-half; Scott was six. They looked so much alike they could have been brothers: dark straight hair, big brown eyes, olive skin. Ryan worshipped Scott, once introducing himself to a neighbor by telling her he was, in fact, Scott.

"But don't tell Scott," he whispered.

Chris and I became fast friends, perhaps because we had adopted children, more likely because Ryan and Scott had more in common than their looks. Scott had rages, too, lashing out at his sisters and parents. Like Ryan, he was maddeningly impulsive. Chris and I would find the two boys up on the garage roof, or holding lit matches to daffodils or kitchen sponges to see if they burned. But also like Ryan, Scott was sweet and earnest, a kid who could break your heart. When Ryan was in first grade, Scott would pull a chair next to Ryan at our kitchen table and take pains to draw a perfect cursive S as an example for his younger friend. He'd help me stir the chocolate chips into the dough and thank me a dozen times for the cookies I sent home with him.

Chris was the first mother with whom I could be completely candid about my son and myself, because she was candid with me. I didn't feel like a loser around her, because despite her Good Mother credentials—quitting her job, cooking wonderful meals every night, beaming so genuinely at the family around her kitchen table—she struggled like I did, at least with Scott. Hers was one of the few homes where I didn't worry about Ryan shocking or offending anyone with his misbehavior, and she felt the same about Scott in our home.

On our long walks through the neighborhood, Chris validated that raising children like Scott and Ryan was exhausting and frustrating. We talked for hours, analyzing our sons, recounting the latest infuriating, worrisome, confounding incidents.

She always ended up making me laugh. She had a sunnier outlook than I did. She was unrelentingly hopeful, even after she discovered that Scott had been physically and emotionally abused for the first three years of his life, even after Scott first talked of suicide at age six, even after he had to leave our local public school in fourth grade to attend a program run by the county mental health department, even after he started a fire in his bedroom. Chris believed completely that our children would turn out okay, that eventually our loving hands would smooth their rough edges and heal their wounds. Whatever deficiencies our kids had, whatever challenges got in their way, they could be fixed.

Anything could be fixed, she always told me.

Several years later on the same exact day, Chris and I found out how wrong she was.

Eight

S chool got worse each year for Ryan. Homework ended in tears and tantrums most evenings. At Ross Middle School, when Ryan had to go from class to class and deal with multiple teachers, he fell apart. He became increasingly frustrated as the homework load and academic difficulty grew. He became agitated at the abruptness with which one class ended and another began. Switching tasks seemed to take a physical toll, as if he were being whacked in the head. His anxiety grew, which made him even more impulsive.

Ryan often interrupted his teachers to ask about instructions they had just delivered or the homework assignments they were still explaining. Sometimes he became belligerent. He began spending longer periods of time in "resource," the euphemism for special ed. It was a small room in which the resource specialist worked with kids who had learning difficulties. Eventually, unable to tolerate the pace and demands of the regular middle school classroom, Ryan became so disruptive that he was spending entire days in the resource room.

We tried medication, as well as homeopathy and behavioral plans and more occupational therapy. But nothing worked. Ritalin gave Ryan tics: he cleared his throat every few seconds; he cracked his elbows by throwing his arms out straight; he hummed. Worst of all, he lost his spark. We stopped the Ritalin, and under the guidance of a behavioral pediatrician, we put him on Neurontin, which can act as a mood stabilizer. But it had little impact and we stopped that, too.

Barry and I were arguing more and more. Ryan's problems seemed the only topic of conversation between us. It didn't help that Ryan took out his worst frustration on me. Barry was always the good guy, the pal, the one Ryan slung his arm around when we were walking down the street, the one he cuddled next to when we watched TV on our bed at night. I resented Barry and his relationship with Ryan. I resented Ryan for preferring Barry to me, though, of course, it made perfect sense. I found myself crying at the smallest provocation, even at work. By this time I had left sports and was writing three columns a week for the op-ed page. As soon as I got home at the end of the day, I just wanted to go to bed. I finally saw a psychiatrist, who prescribed an antidepressant.

I should not have been surprised by the diagnosis of depression. My family tree is lousy with depressives. I can't say how many were actually mentally ill and how many were suffering the effects of being around those who were. All I know is that the vein runs deep, though I had no idea how deep until one night in 1997.

My parents were eating dinner in their Florida dining room when my father's brother Tommy called from California. Tommy was the youngest of my father's seven brothers and sisters and the biggest personality. They had become close as adults when Tommy lived near my parents in Florida for several years. They remained close when Tommy moved back to California. He would fly up to San Francisco whenever my parents visited me, showing up once in a leather suit, though he was an accountant with three adult children.

On the phone that night, Tommy talked about flying to Florida to celebrate St. Patrick's Day with my father. Before he hung up, he had a question.

"Do you know today is Dad's birthday?"

My father said, no, he had not remembered. He found it odd that Tommy had mentioned it. They never talked about their father.

Less than two hours later, the phone rang again. Again it was from California. This time it was Tommy's son, Tom.

He said his father was gone.

"What do you mean gone? Where'd he go?" my father asked.

He's dead, Tom said.

The color drained from my father's face. He sank into his chair.

"That can't be," he said. "I was just talking to him."

Tommy had picked up his dry-cleaning, dropped off a birthday card at his son's apartment, went home, and shot himself. The son said his mother heard the shot as she walked into the house.

Tommy didn't leave a note.

It was only then that I learned what else my father carried from his childhood.

When he was twelve years old, his father, my grandfather, looped a belt around a closet rod in a bedroom of their Bronx apartment. Then he looped it around his neck. My father's fourteen-year-old brother found him. Like Tommy so many years later, he didn't leave a note.

The antidepressants helped me. I no longer felt like I was walking around without skin. I didn't cry over every slight. But my healthier disposition didn't change the fact that there was so much tension in our house that we rarely made it through a night without a blowup.

Ryan's problems began to take a toll on our marriage. Barry and I had different ideas on how to handle our son. I thought Barry was too lenient; he thought I was too harsh. I imagine we were both right, but all we could see was how the other one was making Ryan worse. Sometimes it felt as if we each loved, and were raising, a different son. We'd either be stewing in stony silence, or we'd be examining Ryan's latest incident—a tantrum at school, a failed play date—as if performing an autopsy, every angle examined, every theory tested.

As much as I dreaded the nightly battles over homework, I began to dread even more the debriefings between Barry and me once Ryan went to bed. It felt like we just went around in circles, pointing out the same landmarks over and over, thinking that this time we would notice something we had missed before. The discussion always ended with one or the other of us exhaling in frustration and saying, "I can't talk about this anymore." It was usually me. Barry dealt with his anxiety by talking. I'd finally explode.

"Haven't we been through this a million times?" I'd say.

"I know, but who else am I going to say this to?"

We went to counseling. We loved each other. We even liked each other. But we were lost, spiraling downward in ever tighter circles. The counselor suggested we were responding to Ryan's behavior out of fear: we feared he wouldn't be accepted by his peers, that he wasn't going to be able to live a happy, successful life. Barry's way of playing out his fear was to protect Ryan at all costs. Make sure he never failed. Smooth over bad behavior with a joke or an excuse. My way was to drop the hammer. Ground him. Yell at him. Take stuff away. Make him feel embarrassed enough to change.

During one counseling session, as the therapist got me talking about my family, I recognized for the first time what was really fueling my fear: I was afraid—pit-of-the-stomach, staring-at-the-ceiling-at-midnight afraid—that Ryan was going to turn out like my brother Bobby.

Bobby was a year older than I, the second of the six kids. He was born with a bone missing from his right temple, so his head looked like someone had thrown a baseball into it. He had neu-

rofibromatosis, sometimes referred to as Elephant Man's disease.
(It was later found that John Merrick actually had Proteus syn-
drome, not neurofibromatosis.) Bobby grew benign, fatty tumors
on his skin called neurofibromas and light brown spots that looked
like birthmarks.

My brother, like most children with neurofibromatosis, had
learning disabilities. Bobby couldn't read well and had terrible
handwriting. He had a stunning memory, however, remembering
the birthdays of every aunt and cousin in the family and reciting
facts about planets, prehistoric eras, World War II battles, and
Confederate generals until you wanted to scream.

He had no social skills and thus no friends except us, his
brothers and sisters. And we weren't crazy about him. He always
grabbed the last cookie or elbowed his way to be the first to play
the new air hockey game. He didn't know when to stop teasing,
and once so upset my brother Gerard that Gerard hurled a steak
knife at him. I remember watching Bobby and my brother Kenneth play Ping-Pong one day. I let out a laugh when Bobby badly
missed a return. He took the paddle, and leaning over so he was
within ten inches of me, smashed the ball into my face.

His general weirdness made him a daily target of the school
bullies. Bobby was bullied and harassed every single day. He was
called a retard, a sissy, a fag. He ate lunch alone. He walked home
alone. As if his classmates needed another reason to torture him,
he developed breasts when he hit adolescence, a condition called
gynecomastia. For a year, until he had surgery, he walked stooped
over so that his shirt would hang loosely away from the abomina-
tions on his chest.

I cried many nights for his misery. No one should live like
Bobby did. I prayed and prayed. I believed in prayer then. I wondered why God wouldn't give him just one wonderful thing—a
gift for music, maybe, a sense of humor, a friend of his own.

But every day seemed to bring new humiliations, even as an
adult. Bobby lived near my parents in Florida. The first time he

visited me in California, he was nearly thirty years old and had never traveled out of the Eastern time zone. He worried about jet lag. He worried about the logistics of me picking him up at the airport. He worried about changing planes in Dallas. As he waited for the boarding call in Dallas, he sat in a puddle of spilled soda. Because he had been sure the airlines would lose his baggage, he had brought a change of clothes with him. But when he was changing his pants in the men's room, his wallet slipped out of his pocket unnoticed. So he showed up in San Francisco with no money or credit cards and soiled pants in his carry-on. It was so Bobby.

I couldn't help fearing Ryan might suffer the way Bobby did. I needed Ryan to be strong and brave and independent, stronger than the forces out there trying to beat him down. My son, I knew, was not Bobby. Ryan was loving and gregarious and self-effacing. He was, in fact, independent, and for the most part, fearless. But he wasn't as savvy or as socially adept as other kids. He could be provoked easily. It was enough, I knew, to attract shunning or teasing.

Still, even after my revelation in the counselor's office, I continued to cry in the assistant principal's office, frustrated and sad about news of another outburst, rude remark, or tussle in the playground. But I also was understanding why Ryan did some of the things he did.

Kids with learning differences would rather be perceived as bad than stupid. Nothing is worse than being stupid. So they'll get into fights rather than admit they still don't know the rules to a game that the kids have been playing since first grade. They'd rather get thrown out of the classroom than be exposed as not knowing material everyone else knows.

By the end of Ryan's first year in middle school, Ross School administrators, God bless them, agreed that Ryan needed a different learning environment. They transferred him to Star Academy, a school for kids with learning differences.

Star Academy leased space from a nondescript church on a busy street in San Anselmo, the town next to ours. It had about forty kids, ages seven to nineteen. In this cramped building of narrow hallways and worn carpets, Ryan began to understand for the first time that intelligence is not determined by how well you sit at a desk and memorize facts, or how quickly you process information. His gifted teachers—and speech therapists, art therapist, reading specialists, and occupational therapist—helped him to understand how his own brain worked, and how to shore up his weaknesses and cultivate his strengths. He learned to laugh at his faulty memory and distractibility, his impulsivity and poor organization.

"I tell my friends I'm the best person to tell a secret to," he said one day after school. "Because I never remember what they told me!"

We decided to try meds again. Even in the controlled environment of Star Academy, Ryan couldn't pay attention for more than a few minutes. He couldn't maintain friendships. He was completely impulsive. We found our way to a psychiatrist who specialized in pediatric pharmaceuticals. Giving Ryan meds, he explained, was like giving insulin to a diabetic: the meds were making up for the chemicals his brain wasn't producing in the correct amounts. This time the combination of meds seemed to lift the black cloud inside of Ryan. He was happier, calmer, more engaged. We saw more of his great heart, which Barry always reminded me was Ryan's saving grace.

He was still as obsessive as ever, perhaps more so. For about a year, he cut pictures from magazines every night in bed before he went to sleep. Hundreds and hundreds of pictures, mostly cars and dogs. Ryan just kept cutting and collecting. In the morning, his bedroom floor always looked like it had been hit by a storm of paper scraps. The pictures went into a wire storage bin to be used someday for . . . even he didn't know what.

He kept a meticulous notebook of interesting words he came across in his school readings. Ryan had pages and pages, all of them filled with his cramped print, one word jammed against the next, hundreds on a single page.

"Mom, what does foolhardy mean?"

I'd tell him and out came the notebook. "Foolhardy," he'd print, right below "agnostic" and "teetotaler." He kept another notebook of all the songs he liked on the car radio, pages and pages and pages of artists' names and song titles. Maybe his impulse for external order was a way to control internal disorder. Maybe it was his version of my charts and binders.

Ryan's greatest obsession was cars. He had hundreds of Matchbox cars. He kept his favorites lined up on the kitchen windowsill in a strict order known only to him, and God help anyone who touched one. This child who couldn't remember the days of the week in order knew every make and model of American muscle car ever made. Whenever we were driving, he held forth on the pros and cons of each one we passed. He retrieved free auto sales magazines from newspaper boxes and combed through every page, circling and starring the ones he liked and stacking the magazines on the floor of his bedroom. We kept hoping he would transfer this meticulousness to his schoolwork.

Through Ryan's childhood, we imagined a point somewhere in the distance where all the many tracks of therapies and diagnoses converged. The combination of a new school and new meds brought us closer to that point than we had ever been. It wasn't perfect, by any means, but there was less yelling and stomping and fewer tear-soaked apologies.

Ryan and I had begun to enjoy longer stretches of time without conflict. We loved to travel together, just the two of us. We took car trips to Lake Tahoe, loading the car with junk food we allowed ourselves only on car trips. We would stop a million times—at an interesting town, an antique store, a cute diner, never worrying about "making good time." The two of us spent two weeks in Tanzania with my aunt, a Maryknoll sister who worked with families devastated by AIDS. We stopped in New York on the way, spending an entire day wandering through flea markets in Chelsea and vintage shops in the Village.

On the way home, we were delayed at the Nairobi airport for eight hours and found ourselves laughing so hard and long at a stupid joke Ryan had made up. We already had been chuckling at the memory of Ryan's nephew's attempt at joke-telling. He was four years old. "Why did the pirate's boat sink?" Jared had asked us. We waited for the punch line. "Because," Jared said, "it had a hole in it." The joke became a family legend, prompting new rounds of laughter whenever it was recalled.

In the Nairobi airport, when Ryan and I had become punchy from boredom and fatigue, Ryan launched into a Jared-like joke: "Two guys walk into a bar," he said. "Then they walk out." I laughed so hard the muscles in my face nearly seized up and my throat emitted little piglet sounds, which got Ryan laughing. As soon as one of us stopped laughing, the other would start up, and we'd both be doubled over again. It remains one of my fondest memories of the trip.

Ryan spent ninth grade at Star Academy, then entered a small private high school in Sausalito, repeating ninth grade there. With hard work and good tutors, he passed all his courses and finally began to believe what we had always told him: that he would be a great adult because, unlike school, the real world rewards specialists, not generalists. He had only to find one thing he loved and be great at that.

He already had begun to find it.

When he was thirteen, he often rode his bike to and from Star Academy. Gunning's Hobbies, on San Anselmo Avenue, became a regular stop on Ryan's ride home. He'd check out the model trains and samurai swords and collectible World War II figurines. The couple who owned the place, Alice and Steve, began giving him odd jobs: pricing merchandise, straightening items on the shelves, sweeping the aisles. Soon Ryan was working there a couple days a week. Steve, a curmudgeon with a short fuse, treated

Ryan like a peer. He gave him no quarter for his learning differences. He barked at Ryan in exasperation when Ryan got stuck
on doing something a certain way or didn't follow Steve's directions. Sometimes he simply told Ryan to go home when he'd had
enough. Ryan shrugged off Steve's impatience.

"He's like that to the customers, too," he told us.

Alice thought Ryan was the greatest kid she'd ever met. The
two of them would sit on stools behind the register and have long
conversations. Whenever they said good-bye at the end of the
day, Alice hugged and kissed Ryan and told him she loved him.
Alice and Steve brought out a side of Ryan we hadn't seen. He
wasn't just stocking shelves and organizing storage closets; he
was advising customers on birthday gifts for their grandchildren,
working the cash register, helping to decorate the front window,
even minding the store by himself for short stretches. He was paid
in merchandise. He always took models of classic cars.

Later, when Ryan was sixteen, he got an "internship" (read:
nonpaying job) at Lucky Garage, two blocks from the hobby shop.
By this time, he knew he was good with his hands. He could build
things. For birthdays, he asked for tools: a band saw, a wrench set,
an electric drill, a sander. With them, during the summer of 2006,
between his freshman and sophomore years of high school, he
started making skateboards.

On August 16, 2006, a week before the start of tenth grade,
Ryan fastened new bearings to the wheels of a skateboard he was
building. He had just come home from working at Lucky Garage.
His shirt stuck to his back from sweat. His fingernails were black
with grime and motor oil.

Barry opened our garage door to see what he was doing.

"How about taking a shower?" Barry said, patting Ryan on the
chest. "You smell like a goat."

"I'm not dirty enough yet," Ryan said, smiling. At 6 feet 3
inches tall and 215 pounds, he towered over his father. Barry
laughed.

"Okay, but Mom and I are leaving soon for our meeting at school. Make sure you feed Bill." Bill is our dog.

Barry returned to the house to change his clothes. I was already upstairs getting ready. Ryan left the garage with the skateboard under his arm.

He didn't take a helmet.

PART II

Nine

There was no blood. No obvious injury.

When I drove up to the scene, Ryan was already strapped into a stretcher, surrounded by police and paramedics. Three neighborhood boys had raced to our house on their bikes and knocked on our back door. "Ryan fell off his skateboard," one said breathlessly. "He's on Lagunitas Road." Three blocks away.

Barry and I had been about to leave for the meeting at school to plan the annual fund-raising gala.

I shouted upstairs, where Barry was still dressing.

"Ryan fell off his skateboard," I said. "I'll go check it out."

I drove the three blocks to Lagunitas Road, where a fire truck, an ambulance, and a police cruiser were parked near the stop sign where the road meets Willow Avenue. A small crowd of boys and several adults—residents and passersby—had gathered around Ryan. He was on a stretcher on the ground, straining against the belts pulled tight across his chest, thighs, and forehead. He had an immobilizing collar around his neck. He had been stripped to his boxer shorts. He had a scrape by his left eye and another scrape near the crown of his head. He kept trying to wrest himself free of the straps and grew increasingly irritated that he couldn't.

One of the boys later told me he saw Ryan on his skateboard gaining speed down a long slope on Lagunitas Road. Ryan began to wobble—perhaps he hit a rock, perhaps the new bearings on his wheels malfunctioned. He lost control, flying forward off the board. His bare head slammed into the road, then hit several more times as he rolled. He came to rest, face down, near the stop sign at Willow Avenue. The boy ran to Ryan and called 911 as soon as he saw Ryan was crying. He had never seen Ryan cry.

The paramedic crouching over Ryan said he had no broken bones, but because he had hit his head, they were taking him to the hospital to be checked.

"Are you all right, sweetie?" I asked, kneeling next to him.

He said the right side of his head was the only place that really hurt.

"He wasn't wearing a helmet," the police officer said. He knew Ryan, as all the officers did, not because Ryan got into trouble but because he always stopped to chat and listen to their stories.

"As soon as he's fixed up, I'm going to kill him," I joked.

The officer laughed. "If I don't get to him first."

My stomach didn't lurch. My heart didn't stop. I didn't feel what I had always heard you felt in the moment that your life changes.

I wasn't worried, in part because I knew rescue teams in our little town roar to the scene when old Mr. Pitts steps off the curb too hard while walking his Yorkshire terrier. And I am my mother's daughter. She wasn't much for kissing away tears when we fell from trees or bobbed up sputtering from a dive into the deep end. "What were you doing there in the first place?" she'd ask. If we hurt ourselves on the ball field, she didn't move from her seat in the stands. She figured if the injury was bad enough, someone would summon her.

I raised Ryan similarly, in that I knew the odds were heavily in my favor that he would survive, no matter what stupid stuff he did. I was probably, by today's standards, an underprotective mom. I believed fear was, generally speaking, a useless expenditure of energy. I knew the newspapers were filled with murders and grisly accidents. But I also knew, because I was a reporter, that these awful things were out of the norm. That's why they were in the paper. The odds are always in the favor of nothing bad happening.

The paramedics loaded Ryan into the ambulance and handed me his jeans, T-shirt, and sneakers. I told them my husband and I would meet them at Marin General, less than four miles away. I called Barry on my cell to tell him what was happening and that I would be by in about a minute to pick him up.

"I heard sirens," he said when he climbed into the car.

"His head hurts, so they're going to get him checked out," I said.

Fifteen minutes later, at around 5:45 in the afternoon on a sunny Wednesday, Barry and I pulled into the parking lot of Marin General. Ryan had been there only one other time, for another skateboard mishap. He had fallen going down a hill, ripping the skin from his right arm and leg. That time he was wearing a helmet.

I reached into the backseat and gathered up Ryan's clothes. He would need them for the ride home. But at the last moment, I tossed them back into the car. If he has a concussion, I thought, they might need to keep him overnight. I could always dash out to the car if he was given the okay to leave.

The waiting room was empty. We filled out paperwork and took seats in front of the aquarium. I wondered if I should call the school to say why we were missing the meeting. Barry and I stared at the fish. Then we stared at the TV mounted on the wall in the corner. There was a news story about Google providing the town of Mountain View with free wireless Internet.

Fifteen minutes passed. Thirty.

The last time Ryan had been there, I was in the treatment room the entire time. I asked the receptionist why we couldn't go back to see Ryan. He said he'd check. Finally a white-haired doctor appeared from behind the automatic double doors. He said Ryan was still being settled, that someone would come get us soon. Okay. Thanks. I checked my watch. How long does it take to settle one kid?

Another fifteen minutes.

Then a middle-aged woman emerged from the double doors. She asked if we were Ryan's parents. I looked at the job title on her nametag.

Chaplain.

Ten

The woman walked us out of the waiting room, down a short hallway, and into her office.

"What's going on?" I asked, my heart pounding. "Why are we talking to a chaplain?"

She said a whole team is summoned when there is a "full trauma." A surgeon, an anesthesiologist, a chaplain. She listed others that I don't remember now.

"What do you mean a full trauma?" Barry asked.

"He bumped his head," I said.

The chaplain leaned forward in her chair, her elbows on her knees. She said she wished she had more information for us. A doctor would talk to us soon.

The doctor knocked lightly on the door before entering. It was the same one who had come to the waiting room. He looked shaken. He didn't sit. He said Ryan had sustained a significant head injury. He had been put into a drug-induced coma.

He led us down the hall into the large ER hub with counters and computers in the center and curtained rooms along the walls.

The doctor pulled back a curtain. Ryan was in a blue hospital gown. His long body filled the bed. His head was wrapped in white gauze. He had a thick tube protruding from his mouth; it was attached to a machine that was helping him breathe. Two IVs snaked from his arms and connected to clear bags of liquid hanging from a metal stand. There was blood on the sheet under Ryan's right elbow, where, we later learned, he had yanked out one of the IVs. Nurses scurried around him with tubes and needles and sterile things in sealed packets.

Barry and I stood there, mute, trying to take it in.

A drug-induced coma? A ventilator? Ryan had fallen off a skateboard, for God's sake. He had been conscious and even talking. How could he suddenly be like this?

The doctor explained that during the ambulance ride Ryan had become disoriented and agitated, classic signs of a traumatic brain injury. The EMTs had called the hospital en route to elevate his case to a full-activation trauma. He had been sedated to keep him from injuring his head any further and to allow the staff to treat him.

The ER doc took us to a computer on a counter outside Ryan's room. On the screen was a CT scan of our son's brain. The doctor pointed to a white blotch; it looked like a bleed, he said. Ryan probably would need surgery. It was a "significant" injury, he said. The neurosurgeon was on his way. He would be able to tell us more.

We returned to Ryan's side. We were trying to gather information, absorb what everyone was saying. I listened to the list of medications. Versed. Dilantin. Lidocaine. I knew them. I had spent much of the previous year chronicling the lives of two young soldiers who lost their legs to improvised explosive devices in Iraq. Both had suffered closed head injuries, and both had been given many of these same meds to put them into comas. The two soldiers had emerged from their head injuries pretty much intact—and they had been blown up. All Ryan did was fall off a skateboard on a suburban street.

So while I was worried and nervous, I didn't panic about seeing him this way. I knew he wasn't in a real coma. I knew he was sedated to reduce the activity among the neurotransmitters, which could further damage the brain tissue. I knew he could be brought out of the coma whenever the doctors wanted. I understood this was standard head injury protocol. It all seemed familiar to me from my time with the two soldiers.

But the people in the ER seemed to be expecting tears, and neither Barry nor I was complying. They kept offering us water and Kleenex in that awful, pitying tone you hear only in funeral parlors and hospitals.

"This is a *significant* injury," the ER doctor said yet again, drawing out his words. He mentioned something called "Cushing's triad" and "burr hole" and "evacuation and closing." He paused. He stared at me, as if trying to discern if I understood what he was telling me.

Then he said, "Is there anyone you want to call?"

I began to cry. Okay, I get it. My son might die. The chaplain, hovering in the background, handed me the box of tissues I had declined earlier.

One of the doctors—perhaps the anesthesiologist—lifted his head from adjusting the tubes in Ryan's arms. He said Ryan's vitals weren't looking good. His heart was spiking, then dropping. He said in his opinion Ryan needed surgery *right away*.

"Do you have other children at home?" he asked.

I looked at him. *Do I have other children at home?*

"No," I said.

No, I wanted to scream at him. No, I don't. This is it. I have no spares at home.

I pulled a small notebook from my purse. The reporter in me kicked in. I flipped the pages and came across a list: "sandwich, snacks, breakfast, water, socks, extra shirt, sunscreen, hat, Aleve."

They were items my friend Lorna had told me to bring on a seventeen-mile hike we took near Lake Tahoe the previous weekend. Could that have been just five days ago?

I turned the page.

"CT scan," I wrote. "Hemorrhage. Evacuation. Versed. Induced coma. 'Do you have other children at home?' Significant. Substantial. Cushing's triad. Bur hole. Evacuating and closing."

The neurosurgeon arrived. Dr. Peter Nguyen looked to be in his forties. He looked at the CT scan, then led us back to the chaplain's office. Yes, he said, it was a significant injury, but it didn't require surgery at the moment. He was soft spoken and reassuring. They would monitor Ryan closely for any changes.

We bounded out of the office and back to Ryan's side. I stroked his arm.

"Sweetie, you're going to be fine," I said.

Minutes later, Dr. Nguyen reappeared. He needed to talk to us again. We stepped outside. He said he had not seen the full set of X-rays. Ryan's CT scan was on the screen. He pointed to the same white splotch the ER doc had shown us.

It was a significant bleed. The pool of blood was pressing on Ryan's brain. Dr. Nguyen explained the specifics. I remember none of them. I remember only that he delivered the diagnosis in a way that left no wiggle room. Ryan needed surgery now to stop the bleeding.

A nurse handed us a clipboard. Barry and I signed the forms.

We went back to Ryan. There was a fluttering of preparation. New IVs being snapped into place. I held Ryan's still hand. His nails were black from the garage and from putting the new bearings on his skateboard. I traced his eyebrows with my finger. I lifted his hand and kissed it, then Barry did the same.

"You're going to be fine, Bucko," he said.

Then they wheeled him away.

I went outside to the parking lot and called my parents in Florida.

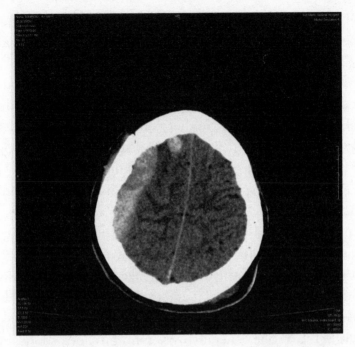

CT scan the day of Ryan's accident, August 16, 2006. The shadow on the left side of scan—which is the right side of Ryan's head—shows the accumulation of blood in his brain.

"Ryan had a skateboard accident and hit his head," I said, trying to modulate my voice.

We were not a family that cried. We did our celebrating and fighting at the top of our lungs but our suffering in silence. There was an assumption that life was hard for everybody, and you soldiered on.

"I'm sure he's going to be all right," I said. "But he's in surgery. Say some prayers."

I said this out of habit. I long ago had stopped believing in prayer. Despite a childhood of Sunday masses and Saturday confessions and long afternoons of catechism classes, I had come to distrust what people called faith. Maybe I had reported on too many exploitive ideologues and fanatics. Religious faith smacked of primitivism and magical thinking. I believed in facts, numbers, source materials. I believed in medical expertise, sophisticated equipment, well-tested pharmaceuticals.

Barry and I sat alone in the surgical waiting room on the second floor. I picked up *People* magazine. I put it back down. I couldn't read anything. Neither could Barry. We could barely speak. This was really happening. Our son was in an operating room and a doctor was drilling into his skull.

I fished my phone out of my purse again and called Lorna. I wanted her with me.

Lorna and I had met when Ryan and her daughter, Emma, were in kindergarten together. Unlike most of the mothers waiting outside school at 2:30 every day, she looked as unpolished as I did most days, though she pulled it off better. She had a willowy build with legs like a dancer's. She rarely bothered to put on makeup or style her hair. She generally wore running shoes, shorts, and a tank top. She usually had come from a run or a hike, or from her art studio, and she still had paint or cement under her fingernails. No tennis skirts. No kitty heels. No scarves. She didn't try to put up a good front. When Emma wailed and carried on almost every morning of kindergarten, distraught that her mother was leaving, Lorna shrugged and smiled.

"I'm so proud," she'd joke.

We got to know each other through a Thursday morning hiking group. As a newspaper columnist, my schedule was flexible enough to escape into the hills near my house once or twice a week. Lorna and I would end up talking for two hours straight, barely noticing the other twenty women navigating the trail with us. Lorna was a sculptor who usually had several projects going at once, fitting her work time around her kids' schedules. She had grown up in Wellesley, Massachusetts, met her husband at Union College in New York, then earned a master's in fine arts at Columbia. She taught art for years, several in Harlem. She moved to

Northern California when her husband, Doug, took a job with an investment banking company in San Francisco.

Lorna and Doug lived a few blocks away from Barry and me, so their family and ours fell into the habit of having dinner together at least once a week, usually twice and sometimes three times. We would run into each other at the corner grocery and end up at one house or the other, grilling chicken and tossing Caesar salads. Doug and Barry were both passionate cooks and went to elaborate lengths to prepare exquisite dinners on the weekends, shopping at the farmers' market, marinating, chopping, seasoning, braising. At our Christmas Eve gift exchange every year, the two men bought each other cookbooks.

Both men traveled frequently: Doug to visit companies in which he had invested, Barry to sporting events across the country. The downside to working as a sportscaster was being away from home several nights a week, though Barry's schedule had improved in recent years. He left ESPN to work for Fox because Fox assigned him to Pac-10 football and basketball, which meant most of his trips were short flights to West Coast cities.

When our husbands were away, Lorna and I and our kids got together for simple, communal meals of store-bought roasted chicken and maybe some cheese and crackers. And always a bottle of wine. Emma and her older brother, Ben, became like cousins to Ryan. Our two families traveled together to Kenya one year, to Tahiti another. Lorna and I took a trip on our own to Ireland to visit a friend whose husband was shooting a movie on location there. Lorna and Doug owned a condo at the edge of the ski resort at Squaw Valley near Lake Tahoe, and the place became something of a second home for us, too. Barry and I didn't ski, but Ryan was crazy for snowboarding.

In the surgical waiting room that night, I dialed Lorna's number.

"I'll be right there," she said.

She, Doug, and Emma arrived minutes later. Ben was away at college. Lorna wrapped her arm around my shoulder and I leaned into her. "He's going to be fine," she said. Then, in her practical Lorna way, she called a good friend who is a doctor in San Francisco and took notes about what questions to ask the neurosurgeon.

The surgery took about an hour. Dr. Nguyen said he had removed a silver-dollar-sized portion of Ryan's skull, then suctioned and scraped out the accumulated blood, which was described later to me as like hard Welch's grape jelly. He reattached the disc of bone with titanium rivets.

He said Ryan had sustained "a right linear skull fracture from frontal to sagittal bone, subdural and epidural hematoma, and right frontal contusion." I looked this up later in the hospital records; the words were a blur that night.

The doctor took us into a small room where he showed us the post-op CT scan. I pulled Lorna in with us, certain that neither Barry nor I would be focused enough to take in the details. I saw something on the scan I had not seen on the earlier ones.

There was a clear jagged line cutting across Ryan's skull from the base to the forehead. It's one thing to see a white spot that is supposed to be blood but looks like a smear of bleach on a photonegative. But this crack. This was recognizable, undeniable, sickening.

I suddenly felt light-headed and nauseous, as if I might faint. I could barely breathe. Lorna led me to a chair in the hallway, leaving Barry alone to nod his head at the neurosurgeon's explanations, as if any of this made sense.

The doctor told us there was no reason to spend the night at the hospital. Ryan was in a coma. He was stable. And we lived just six minutes away by car in case anything did happen. We should get some sleep, he told us. We had a long road ahead of us.

We returned home that night to a dark, quiet house. Without Ryan there, the house felt almost creepy, the way abandoned buildings do. There had been only a few nights in Ryan's sixteen years that he wasn't with Barry or me. He had never gone away to camp. Barry and I loved to travel, and Ryan went everywhere with us. It sometimes felt as if we were a single unit, three mismatched people who somehow found each other, bound by ties that had nothing to do with blood.

Eleven

He's drifting in the wrong direction," the neurosurgeon told us.

This was a different neurosurgeon from the one who operated on Ryan that first night. Marin General, we discovered, contracted with three outside surgeons to cover traumas. They rotated in every three weeks, starting on Fridays.

It was Saturday, three days after Ryan's accident. Barry was supposed to be broadcasting an Evander Holyfield fight in Las Vegas. Instead he was with me in the ICU waiting room, trying to figure out what exactly this doctor was telling us. His name was Mark Eastham, and he had just started his weeklong shift the day before, taking over for Dr. Nguyen.

Ryan had seemed to be doing okay on Thursday and Friday. His CT scans had shown no worsening of the bleed. His nurse had passed along to us several signs that Ryan's brain was rebooting: he was pulling at his breathing tube and he had scratched his nose on the way to one of his scans. I had held a pink plastic vomit pail under his mouth as he threw up on Thursday, less than twenty-four hours after the injury, another sign that his bodily functions were working okay.

Now Eastham was saying that Ryan's brain was still swelling. Swelling normally subsides within seventy-two hours. It had been more than seventy-two hours, and Ryan's swelling was getting worse. Dr. Eastham said the bruises on the right side of Ryan's brain were "blossoming," meaning the bleeds were spreading and exacerbating the swelling.

When the brain swells, Eastham explained, it pushes against the skull. He said to think about getting hit in the eye. The tissue around the eye can swell up as much as it wants because the skin is elastic. The skull is hard and fixed. There is no give. The more the brain swells, the more the pressure builds inside the skull. This is measured by a fiber-optic intracranial pressure (ICP) probe, which had been threaded through a hole drilled into Ryan's skull during his emergency surgery Wednesday night. Normal ICP is 10 or under. Anything over 15 is worrisome. Ryan's ICP had hit 20 and was climbing.

If the pressure gets too high, the blood vessels are squeezed to the point of closing. The parts of the brain deprived of oxygenated blood can be irreversibly damaged; without oxygen, brain cells begin to die within six minutes. Too many compressed vessels can cause death. Uncontrolled pressure causes half of all brain injury deaths among patients who arrive at the emergency room alive.

The swelling also can cause the brain to shift this way or that, destroying the delicate balance of brain, blood, and cerebrospinal fluid. Doctors have two primary treatments for reducing the swelling, as I understood it later: they can drain fluid through a tube inserted through the skull and into the brain, or they can shrink the brain tissue with dehydrating medications like Mannitol and Lasix. Dr. Eastham took the dehydration route. It was less invasive than drilling another hole into Ryan's skull and inserting a drain, which would put Ryan at greater risk of infection. He figured he could insert a drain later if necessary.

Controlling the pressure required a complex manipulation of the body's mechanics. Eastham had to dehydrate the brain enough to minimize swelling, but he had to keep it infused with enough blood to deliver oxygen to every part. This, however, worked at cross-purposes with the need to minimize Ryan's brain activity. The coma-inducing drugs slowed not just brain function but all bodily functions, including his heart; it wasn't pumping hard enough to keep the brain properly infused. So Ryan needed blood pressure meds—just the right dose to pump enough blood to infuse the brain but not enough to exacerbate the swelling. All day and night, Eastham and the ICU nurses adjusted the meds to maintain an almost impossible balance.

Eastham was a rugged, frenetic guy from a hardscrabble neighborhood in Lowell, Massachusetts. He loved the Red Sox, his wife, and his work. He had no children. He wore a T-shirt and sport jacket instead of a white doctor's coat. His clothes were always a little rumpled, his hair a little too long, his face a ruddy red. His eyes were piercing and there was a sense of barely contained energy about him. He gave the impression of always drumming his fingers or tapping his foot, though he did neither. Whenever he talked to us about a CT scan or a surgical procedure, he had the habit of running his hand through his hair and saying, "Does that make sense?" He thought out loud and explained everything. He treated us as people who were dealing with the situation instead of as delicate parents in need of protection and coddling.

I liked him right away.

We had established a base camp in the lobby outside the ICU on the second floor. On the morning after the accident, Lorna had called my closest friends to let them know what had happened, and from there word spread quickly. Friends and neighbors and coworkers streamed in and out all day, delivering pastries and fruit, balloons and cards, keeping us company as we waited for the swelling to subside so we could take Ryan home. I still had his clothes in the backseat.

I led visitors into Ryan's ICU room and was always surprised when I heard the short intakes of breath as they took in the sight: the gauze turban, the hard C-spine collar, the nasogastric tube in his nose, the endotracheal tube clamped to his mouth, a triple lumen subclavian line, a radial arterial line, the bruise by his left eye, the swollen left arm, the hanging bags delivering dopamine, Neo-Synephrine, Versed, fentanyl, propofol, fosphenytoin, Zosyn.

As visitors looked on—trying to hide their shock, they told me later—I'd kiss Ryan's hand and stroke his arm and smile down at him. To me, he looked so peaceful and sweet, the way he did as a baby.

One friend said later I scared her with how calm I was. I wasn't behaving like my usual self: compiling information, making lists, tracking down experts. She worried that I was in such deep denial I might not be capable of making smart decisions. Another friend said I had never looked more beautiful.

"You glowed," she told me later. "Like a new mother."

I don't know why I looked like that. Maybe it was that everything in my life—writing my column, paying bills, answering e-mails—had dropped away. Perhaps for the first time ever I was giving myself over to being wholly and completely Ryan's mother.

Even when Ryan was a baby, I don't think I glowed with utter devotion to being this child's mother the way it seemed my sisters and my friends did with their babies. Maybe I didn't glow over my newborn because I couldn't allow myself to feel like a mother until he was actually in my arms. Because his adoption—any adoption, really—was not a sure thing, I hadn't decorated his room with trains or butterflies. I hadn't bought baby clothes. No one threw me a shower. And, even though I didn't want to think about it, Ryan wasn't legally ours until he was six months old and a judge signed the papers. Maybe with such a tentative beginning, I never gave myself over completely to him.

All I knew was that when I looked down at Ryan in his hospital bed, with his tubes and wrapped head, I saw a child who would soon wake up and need his mother.

Twelve

Eastham's warnings about Ryan's swelling brain had us glued to the green numbers on the electronic ICP monitor next to Ryan's bed.

"What's the ICP now?" everyone asked on Saturday when Barry or I or one of our friends emerged from Ryan's room. All through that morning and into the afternoon, his ICP was in the low 20s. It was high, but it had stopped climbing.

Lorna made a latte run after lunch, and when she returned, she was clutching a copy of that day's *Marin Independent-Journal*, our local paper.

"I know you'll want to see this," she said.

On the front page was a police mug shot of Scott, Ryan's childhood friend, the son of my friend Chris. Scott, who was eighteen, had been arrested in Truckee, near Lake Tahoe, where Chris and her husband, Eric, owned a second home. Scott was being charged with involuntary vehicular manslaughter in the death of another teenaged boy. The boy apparently had assaulted Scott a week earlier and was rushing at Scott's car, which was idling on the street. Scott said he panicked. He hit the gas and hit the boy. Then he kept going, pulling over down the block. Upset and shaken, he called his mother. She told him to call 911 immediately. Scott had no idea the boy had died.

Scott's incident happened the same day as Ryan's.

My stomach dropped. I imagined Chris and Eric looking at their son's mug shot in the paper. He still looked like Ryan: dark hair and eyes, handsome open features. He still looked like a baby. I called Chris right way.

"Chris, call me when you're up to it," I said after the beep. "I can't imagine what you're going through. We're dealing with our own crisis with Ryan. I can't believe this is happening. Call me."

Maybe Scott's situation made me less willing to grasp what Eastham was telling us on that Saturday. If the brain continued to swell, Eastham said, he might have to remove part of Ryan's skull to create room for the swelling.

We were having none of it. Barry and I truly believed that Ryan would be fine. He had rarely been sick. He had never needed antibiotics. He had never broken a bone. He had such a high pain threshold that he grimaced but said nothing while a nurse methodically plucked gravel from his raw wounds after his previous skateboard accident. He was the strongest kid we knew.

I began on that day to call Eastham "Dr. Doom." He was a worst-case-scenario guy. Barry and I were best-case-scenario.

"It's your job as a doctor to worry about all the bad things that might happen," I said. "It's our job as his parents to believe in our son."

By Saturday evening, Ryan's ICP began to drop. He seemed finally to have stabilized.

"See?" I said to Eastham. "Ryan just has to do everything the hard way."

We grabbed at any little uptick like a towrope, happily riding as far as it would take us.

"He's not out of the woods yet," Dr. Doom said.

I smiled. I told him he was at a disadvantage in predicting how all this would play out. He didn't know Ryan and we did.

That night, we went out to dinner with Barry's daughter and her two children. They had flown up from LA. I held the younger son, Jared, on my lap for most of the night, enjoying the weight and warmth against my body. I chatted with Jared and his brother, Kyle, about what movies we should rent because Ryan would be awake soon. I talked as if Ryan were in for a tonsillectomy and in danger of nothing more serious than boredom. It was as if I had pulled a shade down over a window so I couldn't see the storm clouds outside.

Soon after we arrived at the hospital Sunday morning, Ryan's ICP spiked again, up to an unimaginable 30. I didn't know until much later that when an ICP reaches 30, it can mean an escalation of pressure that no medication or surgery can reverse. An ICP of 30 can signal impending death. We only knew that Ryan was in trouble.

Lorna and Doug rushed over, summoned by another friend who saw the almost panicked look on Dr. Doom's face. He told us he was bombarding Ryan with more diuretics and more sedatives.

Once again, the meds stabilized the rising pressure. Ryan was okay, but the day had exhausted us. We trudged out the door that night feeling more defeated than usual and agreed to have dinner with Lorna and Doug, and another close friend, Jeff Appleman, and his son, Josh. We didn't care where we went, we said, as long as it had a full bar.

By Monday, Ryan's ICP still had not dropped as much as Eastham had hoped. He had told us to pull up chairs next to him at the nurse's station inside the ICU. He typed in Ryan's name on the desktop computer. There was a complication beyond the rising pressure, he said. He ran his hand through his hair.

"You see that?" Eastham said, pointing at a line on Ryan's CT scan.

Even our untrained eyes could see that the line between the
two hemispheres of Ryan's brain was bowed toward the left. The
bruises on the right side had swelled so much that they were shoving the brain off midline. The brain stem, like the skull, has no
give, Eastham explained. It's as immovable as a tree trunk. So as
the brain moves to one side, it creates a torque on the blood vessels connecting it to the brain stem. The vessels can shear and
cause irreparable damage, or death.

We didn't grasp all this at the time. All we understood was
that Eastham quickly had to reduce the swelling and reverse the
midline shift. The first surgical option, and the simplest, was to
drain fluid from the brain. Eastham would have to insert a tube
into one of the brain's two lateral, or main, ventricles. These ventricles are kidney-shaped cavities that hold cerebrospinal fluid,
which continuously carries nutrients through the brain and down
the spinal cord. Removing some cerebrospinal fluid would reduce
the overall volume of matter inside the skull, thus relieving pressure and, hopefully, easing the midline shift.

But Eastham couldn't use a drain. The swelling had squeezed
the right ventricle shut; there was no fluid there to drain. And the
fluid in the left ventricle was actually serving as a bulwark, keeping the brain from pushing even farther toward the left side.

The next option was the one we had instinctively rejected
several days earlier. Now there was no choice: Eastham would
have to remove part of Ryan's skull.

He explained that it would allow the brain to swell up and
out, like bread rising in a pan, relieving the pressure inside the
skull and diminishing the risk of brain damage. The cranium is
made up of seven bones. The two directly above the brain, acting
as a roof, are the parietal bones. Eastham would remove the one
on the right side. Then, Eastham said, he would sew Ryan's scalp
back in place, laying it directly on the dura, the thickest of the
three membranes that encase the brain. The removed bone flap,
as the piece of skull is called, would be stored in a refrigerated

tissue bank until Ryan's brain had healed. Then it would be reattached with titanium rivets.

As we waited to sign the consent form for surgery, an ICU staffer tapped me on the shoulder. She looked familiar, but I couldn't place her.

"It's Buffy," she said. "From Fallen Leaf."

Buffy and her husband, Slim, lived in the house between ours and Chris's when we lived on Fallen Leaf. Ryan was four when we moved in. Buffy and Slim had no children, and Ryan loved hanging out with them, in part because Slim was a contractor and had great tools.

Buffy handed me a small package wrapped in tissue paper and ribbon. Inside was a tiny misshapen ceramic dish. It was painted green. In the bowl lay a crystal. Buffy said Ryan had made the dish in kindergarten for her, and she had kept paper clips in it on her desk. I never knew Ryan had made her a gift. The crystal was Buffy's. Someone had given it to her when she needed healing, and now she wanted us to have it.

I hugged her, cried, and slipped the dish and crystal into my purse so that it would be with me in the surgical waiting room on the second floor. Lorna and Doug waited with us. I couldn't help rising every few minutes to peer through the windows of the double doors leading to the operating rooms. I tried not to picture the saw buzzing into my son's skull or the flaps of his scalp pulled back.

Today is just today. It is what it is.

Eastham pushed through the door, his surgical cap still on, and said Ryan's ICP already had dropped to between 10 and 15. His brain was soft to the touch, confirming the decreased pressure.

Ryan's swollen brain finally had room to breathe.

"Look," Eastham said, showing us the post-op CT scan. The brain had shifted somewhat to the right. It wasn't back at midline yet but clearly was moving in the right direction.

"It's better. But we're not out of the woods yet."

I smiled. "Do you feel you're not doing your job if you don't say that?"

"I'm just telling you," he said, smiling now, too. He was relieved.

The next morning, Tuesday, we arrived to find Ryan's ICP still in the teens. Perfect. The surgery was doing exactly what everyone had hoped. I stood at his bed, lightly scratching his arms, stroking his cheek, lifting his fingers to my lips to kiss them. I still refused to let the nurses clean the grease from his fingernails.

In the first week at Marin General, our world had shrunk to the size of Ryan's ICU room and the second-floor lobby. Barry and I fell into a daily routine. We'd wake while it was still dark, impatient to get back to Ryan. We'd feed the dog, get the newspapers, unclip the cell phones from the chargers, make sure I had my notebook. We'd drive to the hospital without the radio.

Lorna would show up by nine with lattes and maple scones. Through the day, Barry and I barely finished one latte when a friend stepped off the elevator with two more. I began to save the paper cups, writing the time and date near the rim. The tower of cups would be my way of showing Ryan how much time had passed while he was asleep.

The lobby became our living room and our town square. Friends streamed through all day to sit and talk and keep us company as we waited for Ryan to heal enough to be awakened from his coma. They piled the coffee table with muffins and fruit and almonds and chocolate. Around midday, someone would make a sandwich run. Then the after-school crowd would arrive, then the after-work crowd. One friend said the atmosphere sometimes seemed more like a cocktail party than an ICU waiting room. Maybe. But I liked having people around me. So did Barry. They made us feel safe, insulated. They were like stones in a wall that would help us keep the bad things out.

Lorna became the unofficial mother of our growing waiting room tribe. She took over, but in a way barely felt, like a car changing gears so smoothly and with such precise engineering you don't notice. She seemed to anticipate what we needed and took care of it out of sight. She separated the gawkers from the friends. She intercepted one woman who emerged from the elevator and breathlessly said, "I was told if I wanted to see Ryan alive, I better get over here now!" She guided the nonstop talkers to a corner where she listened so I wouldn't have to. She pulled one woman aside to suggest I definitely was not ready to hear how death was just another state of existence.

Lorna was unfailingly kind and patient and graceful, handling people without them ever knowing they were being handled. She answered the calls on my cell phone to relieve me of delivering the same information over and over. And every night when she returned home, she fielded more calls, everyone wanting to know what they could cook ("Nothing. They don't want to eat at home right now"), what they could do ("Walk the dog. Water the plants. Sit with them in the waiting room").

As the days passed, Lorna was also answering another question: "Why aren't they moving him to UCSF?"

University of California at San Francisco was one of the top hospitals in the country. It, along with San Francisco General, was where the really serious cases went. The cancer kids. The kidney transplants. The crushed chests. We didn't consider moving. We thought we were okay where we were. Maybe we thought that as long as we were at the community hospital, a place of broken wrists and twisted ankles, Ryan's injury could not be all that bad. He was going to be okay. His clothes were still in the back of the car waiting for him.

There was a strange comfort to spending all day in those sofas and chairs. The future and past ceased to exist. We lived suspended in the bubble of that furniture and those double doors, separate from everyday life and everyday responsibilities. It was as if we were drugged: calmed and flattened by the flood of numbing chemicals our brains pumped out as fast as they could, doing their best to protect us from fully registering the horror of what was happening.

Instead of feeling thick and heavy, I felt a strange lightness. Barry said the same thing. Instead of adding stress, the trauma lifted away all the other stresses in our lives. Barry and I were almost always in good spirits, convinced that Ryan would be fine. We joked with Eastham about the Red Sox–Yankees series that week and how we were rooting hard for the Sox so that he would be in a good mood.

Maybe we were, as friends later suggested, in denial. If so, Barry and I were in it together. We were told that trauma to a child can strain a marriage, just as raising a difficult child can. But for some reason—maybe because we already had been through so much with Ryan—Barry and I moved through each day at the hospital as if in a dance, mirror images of calm and practicality, sociability and confidence. We held each other at night, saying little, until we fell into dreamless sleep. We were able, with remarkably little effort, to live in the moment, to keep out thoughts of what *might* happen. We didn't dwell on what we couldn't change, in particular the tempo and course of Ryan's recovery. Every illness and injury, the hospital staffers told us, has its own rhythm. With every report of bad news, Barry and I took to reminding each other:

Today is just today. It is what it is.

We also took to heart the advice an ICU doctor shared with us during those first days. He said we should think of ourselves as setting out on an ocean voyage. We would be facing storms and squalls. The only way to survive, he said, is to keep your ship strong. We had to keep ourselves healthy, he told us. Eat well every day and get a good night's sleep at home. Too many parents, he said, spent twenty-four hours a day at the hospital and ended up getting sick and were of no use to their children.

So we acquiesced when friends pulled us along for walks on the nearby bike trail. The wild grasses along the trail were pale yellow from the long dry summer and seemed to be in a holding pattern, alive but not fully so, waiting for the winter rains. At night, our friends refused to let us go home without feeding us, no matter how worn out we felt. We would kiss Ryan and say good night and tell him we loved him. We called the ICU and talked to the night nurse before we went to sleep to check on his ICP. And when we hung up, Barry always looked at the phone and said, "Don't ring."

I didn't think about how others must have seen me those first few days. I was so practical. So calm. I slept. Ate. Walked. Dealt with everything so logically. Not like a mother with a son in a coma. One of Ryan's ICU nurses, Jimette, was a widow who had a son about Ryan's age. "I didn't know how you could leave him," she told me later. "If it were me, you wouldn't be able to tear me away from him. You must have really trusted us."

I had figured that the way to get people to do their best was to let them do it, and lavish them with muffins and cookies and gratitude. This is not to say I stood back passively. I am soothed by information, or perhaps more accurately by the act of collecting information. It is why, I imagine, I became a reporter. It gives me the illusion of control, of staying on top of things. At the hospital, I asked questions and took notes during our frequent meetings with Eastham.

Yet for all my meticulous documentation of meds and doses and procedures, I was beginning to understand for the first time the concept of faith: real, true faith. But it wasn't in God.

The faith I was discovering in that waiting room outside the ICU was in Ryan himself. Despite what I could see with my own eyes, despite what the doctors told me and what I wrote in my notebooks, I seemed to believe in a magic that would make Ryan whole. And I seemed to believe that Ryan carried that magic within him.

I was only partly right.

Every day, Barry and I received word of the hundreds of prayers being said for Ryan, many from people who we had never met but who knew someone who knew Ryan. Even Evander Holyfield called to tell Barry he was keeping Ryan in his prayers. I began to think of the prayers as units of energy instead of as notes to God. I pictured them streaming into the hospital's main lobby, riding the elevator, swirling around Barry and me, slipping through the double doors of the ICU and seeping into Ryan's skin like the tiny men he used to believe lived inside of him. The tiny men, Ryan once explained, had swimming pools and playgrounds, and they climbed ladders from his feet up to his stomach and head. When I looked at Ryan in his ICU bed, I liked to imagine the tiny men hustling around Ryan's wounded brain, stitching up a ripped synapse here, spackling a weakened blood vessel there.

This warm stream of energy, thought, prayer—whatever name it went by—was so palpable I could almost hold it in my hands.

On that Tuesday morning, one day after Eastham performed the craniectomy to relieve the pressure on Ryan's brain, Barry and I and our friends were in an almost celebratory mood. We had come through the worst of it. There were about six of us in the waiting area, chatting and drinking coffee, speculating about when Ryan might come home. A friend from our little town of Ross stepped off the elevator and walked slowly toward us. She looked ashen.

She had news about a woman we all knew, one of the Good Mothers. The woman had four children, all teenagers. She was attractive and blond and trim. She ran the trails around Phoenix Lake every day. I'd see her on my hikes. She'd wave and smile. She always smiled. She was married to a successful surgeon. Like my friend Chris, she had quit her job to raise her children. I'd see her ferrying them in the family station wagon to soccer and music lessons and tutors. She delivered cupcakes to the classroom on her children's birthdays and served on committees for the various school fund-raisers. Her son and Ryan were in the same grade. She was a mama-bear type, fiercely protective. I remember her son and mine got into a tussle in third or fourth grade. Suddenly the smile was gone and she was making clear that Ryan had better keep his distance. But the next day and for every day thereafter, the smile was back.

In the Marin General lobby, we made room on the couch for my friend from Ross. She delivered the stunning news: the woman we all knew, the mother of four, had jumped off the Golden Gate Bridge the previous afternoon.

I couldn't speak.

That woman? That mother?

Though there was no shortage of speculation, I don't know what compelled her on that particular day to drive to the bridge, park her car, walk onto the span, climb the railing, and let go. Even with my own history of depression, I couldn't imagine such howling darkness. But I wondered about failure, and about me and Chris and this woman, and maybe all mothers.

Chris had tried to do everything right. She loved her child completely. She provided as idyllic a home life as anyone I've ever known. She had gotten Scott the help he needed, even when it meant sending him to a therapeutic school out of state. She was energetic and optimistic. And still Scott ended up in jail, responsible for the death of another human being. And Chris, like every mother I know, stared at the ceiling at night wondering what she should have done differently.

The woman who jumped off the bridge also seemed to have done everything right. We are such idiots. We think everyone else has it all figured out. But we're all stumbling around in dark rooms bumping into the furniture and stifling our cries so no one will know.

As I listened to more details of the suicide from subsequent visitors that morning, I wondered what doctors might have found if they had done a CT scan on the mother's brain that day, before she reached the bridge. Would her brain have shown some mark, some telltale sign, indicating the awful act she was about to commit?

I thought about the CT scans we had seen of Ryan's brain. It should be an amazing thing to peer through someone's skull and into his brain, to see all the wrinkles on the surface, the ventricles, the brain stem. But it wasn't amazing, at least no more amazing than seeing a femur or an ulna on an X-ray. I had long wished to see inside my son's head, to see what combination of chemicals and nerves explained his quirks and gifts, his frustrating behavior and his remarkable sensitivity. And now I finally had pictures of his brain, and they yielded not a single answer.

I remembered a quote I had come across once in researching a story for the newspaper. It was from brain surgeon Roger Sperry, who said, "In the human head there are forces within forces within forces, as in no other cubic half-foot of the universe that we know."

There are thousands of chemical reactions per second in the brain involving 100 billion specialized cells and 100 trillion connections. To fuel all this activity, the brain consumes 20 percent of the body's oxygen and energy, though it makes up only 2 percent of the body's weight.

How could these amazing machinations—all the circuitry that defines our very being—hide so completely from the scanner? If the brain is the seat of human consciousness, storing memories and controlling emotions, if personality and humor and intelligence are products of the physical working of the brain, where were they on the CT scans? Where, among the billions of neurons inside this three-pound lump of fibers and membranes, was my son's mind?

Thirteen

Early Wednesday morning, about thirty-six hours after the craniectomy had lowered Ryan's ICP, the pressure began to climb again, inching back toward 20.

"Why is this kid such a pain in my ass?" Eastham said.

"Now what?" Barry asked.

We were gathered once again around the computer at the nurses' station in ICU. Eastham had already removed half of Ryan's skull. He had increased all the meds. What was next?

Eastham showed us a CT scan from that morning. Ryan's brain was still off midline, so he was still reluctant to insert a ventricular drain. Trying to thread a drain through the bruised brain into one of the ventricles might cause damage to parts of the brain that were, right now, perfectly fine. He said he was going to consult by phone with some colleagues.

Barry and I sank into our seats in the lobby. It was still so early that not even Lorna had arrived with coffee yet. We sat in silence. We were starting to understand that catastrophic illness is so much about acceptance. *It is what it is.* But we also believed this: It will change. Just be patient. It will get better.

Lorna and several friends had joined us by the time Eastham

reappeared. He bounded into the lobby, energized. He had a plan. It was unconventional, he said.

Ryan needed "a little siphoning off" of fluid to get him stabilized. So Eastham was going to coax the cerebrospinal fluid to drain out of the brain into the spinal column. He would insert a thin, flexible tube, called a lumbar drain, into Ryan's lower spine. He explained that the cerebrospinal fluid travels through the body like a chain of lakes: it moves from the two large lateral ventricles in the brain down to the smaller third and fourth ventricles and then down the spinal canal. Draining the lowest lake—the spinal canal—would draw the fluid from the upper lakes down into the empty space.

It sounded logical to us, even brilliant. We especially liked that Eastham wouldn't have to touch Ryan's brain.

He inserted the drain into Ryan's spine, and just like that, Ryan's ICP number dropped to the low teens.

"He just needed a little tweak," Eastham said, pleased.

When we entered Ryan's room to kiss him good night, Eastham was, in his rapid-fire style, delivering instructions to the night nurse. The tube from the lumbar drain had to stay at a certain height so that it didn't overdrain. She had to watch the monitors carefully to make sure his blood pressure and depth of sedation and ICP and oxygen intake were within certain parameters. The nurse furiously took notes.

"Does that make sense?" Eastham asked her.

The nurse nodded but looked as if she had been struck in the head.

Barry and I exchanged an uneasy glance. I looked at the blinking, whirring machines surrounding Ryan's bed, the various medications dripping through tubes into Ryan's body. One simple miscalculation, one forgotten instruction, one technical glitch— that's all it would take. It was the first time we left the hospital feeling unsettled. But the drain had worked. Ryan's ICP was low.

That was the most important thing.

It turned out it wasn't the most important thing.

Fourteen

Ryan's ICP was at a wonderful 10 or 12 when we arrived the following morning, Thursday. Ryan had been in the hospital eight days. Barry, Lorna, and I were flipping through the latest entries in the book Lorna had started the second day of Ryan's coma. It was a sketchbook of thick white paper. Visitors wrote notes to Ryan, glued get-well cards and sprigs of lavender, drew pictures, pasted photographs. One little boy included a Gummy Bear for Ryan to eat when he woke up. It became more a scrapbook than a visitors' log. I glued in a comic strip. In the first two panels, penguins are swimming happily in the water. The last panel shows an ice floe with a penguin standing in full-body armor who says, "I'm not going in like this, Mom." The mother replies, "Hush, sweetie."

"It's been 93 hours since you closed down Lagunitas with the fire truck, police cars, and ambulance," I wrote underneath the cartoon in purple ink. "93 hours translates, I think, to 27 lattes. . . . I'll have to go to caffeine rehab when all this is over. . . . Love, Mom."

Barry drew a kid on a skateboard in a ridiculously large helmet with a tag that said, "The 2006 Ryan Tompkins Skateboard Protective Helmet—Get One Today!" We were laughing over this when a nurse emerged from ICU. She sat down. She had the look.

She said Ryan's pupil blew.

Blew?

It was fixed and dilated, she said.

We asked what that meant.

It meant something was very wrong, she said. The brain seemed to be heading toward the brain stem.

We didn't understand.

"I just want to prepare you," she said.

Prepare us?

"It could mean brain death."

My heart drummed inside my ears. I looked at Barry. His mouth was slack, his eyes wide and terrified.

"Where's Eastham?" Barry asked.

"On his way. I just talked to him."

"Well, shouldn't we wait until *he* gets here before we panic?" I said to the nurse. My fear was coming out as anger toward this nurse for saying such a hateful thing. Brain death? Who was she to raise such a horrific possibility before the doctor had taken a look for himself? Was she a neurosurgeon? But I knew she wouldn't have said anything unless she had seen this before. I knew this was really, really bad.

Lorna followed the nurse back toward the ICU.

"What are you saying?" Lorna demanded, her voice echoing in the hallway.

"I don't believe in sugarcoating," the nurse replied.

"Are you saying Ryan is going to die?"

"We have to be prepared for the worst."

I followed them through the double doors to Ryan's room. I knew it was our job to be stronger than this injury, to believe so hard and so completely that our faith would surround him with an impenetrable shield. Still, I stood at his bed and cried.

"You can't do this," I said, my lips touching his ear. "I can handle anything. But I can't handle losing you, Ryan. I can't survive that."

Until that moment, I didn't know that I could not survive without him. It seemed almost unbelievable that I had forgotten how intensely I loved him. *I had forgotten.* I had always loved him. I knew that. But how long had it been since I had *felt* it? Since it had enveloped me? Since I had enveloped *him* in it? How much time had I squandered? I thought about the battles. The judgments. The disappointments. The crusty bits of resentments and frustrations I let build up around me like a carapace, providing myself a convenient refuge from his rejections and my failures, hardening whatever motherly instincts I once might have possessed.

Back in the lobby, I slumped next to Barry on the sofa, drained, defeated, terrified. Barry looked half dead himself, his eyes vacant. I lifted his arm and wrapped it around me. He squeezed me. The chaplain appeared. She asked what kind of music Ryan liked. We said everything, without looking up at her. She asked what religion we were. We said we had no religion. She stepped into the ICU, presumably to see Ryan, and I asked Lorna to get rid of her. I heard Lorna down the hall.

"I don't think Joan's ready to turn to religion right now," she said in her lovely way. "Why don't you give me a way to get in touch with you if she changes her mind?"

When Ryan's pediatrician, Bill Gonda, arrived, he looked more afraid than we did. I knew then, if I previously had any doubt, that this truly was bad. (Later, I did a Google search of "fixed dilated pupils outcomes." The first result was a 2001 study from the University of Bonn. Of ninety-nine patients who presented with fixed dilated pupils, 75 percent died. Fifteen percent had "unfavorable" outcomes; they were permanently disabled or in a vegetative state. Only 10 percent made "favorable" recoveries.)

Eastham bolted from the elevator and raced straight past us. He already had booked an operating room. Within minutes, he rushed by again, this time jogging next to a gurney carrying Ryan. I clapped my hand to my mouth. Please, please, please.

I knew Lorna and others were phoning all our closest friends. Drop whatever you're doing. Come now.

I called my parents. They had offered to come out earlier, and I had said, no, there was nothing for them to do. Wait until Ryan is home. That's when I'll need the help.

"You should come now," I told them on the phone from a quiet corner of the lobby. I could barely get the words out. They said they'd be on the first plane in the morning.

Barry and I headed toward the elevator that would take us to the surgical waiting room on the first floor. My friend Jill stepped out just as we were about to get on. She opened her arms and I fell into them, sobbing into her shoulder.

"No, no, don't go there," Jill said over and over, her voice cracking.

On the first floor, Barry and I sank, stunned, into the now-familiar chairs of the surgical waiting room. This was our fourth time in eight days. The draining of the initial bleed. The craniectomy. The lumbar drain. Now this, whatever this would be. I knew the stains on the ceiling tiles. I knew the irritating buzz of the fluorescent lighting. The pastel linoleum floors. The mangled magazines on end tables. The cold vinyl chairs. There was nothing in that room to distract us from the excruciating possibility that Eastham could emerge at any moment from those awful double doors and fumble for words.

Eight or nine friends waited with us, including Ryan's pediatrician. I was told people were collecting upstairs, no one willing to leave until the surgery was over. I pictured everyone talking in low voices, updating the latecomers.

"Tell me a story," I said to my friend Erin as we waited. "Tell me something normal."

I needed to pretend Ryan was by the creek in the backyard, building a makeshift bridge, chasing lizards, throwing rocks. Ryan couldn't be in the operating room on the other side of those double doors. We couldn't be here in this awful room.

Erin just started talking, telling me about her kids not feeding the dog, the Giants game last night, her son's baseball practice, talking as if she were telling me a bedtime story, assuring me there were no monsters under the bed. I was safe as long as she kept talking.

Barry sat with her husband, Rob. Barry's face was gray. He had a three-day growth of beard. His hair, always just so, fell onto his forehead. During a camping trip several years ago, he and Rob had spent an entire weekend telling jokes. Eight hours straight of "A guy walks into a bar . . ." and "So Jesus is talking to his disciples at the Last Supper . . ." Now as I sat with Erin, I heard Barry laugh. Rob was telling jokes. He was doing for Barry what Erin was for me: lifting him out of this room for a moment, transporting him somewhere else, maybe to the Mendocino campsite. Anywhere but here.

I don't remember how long Ryan was in surgery. Forever.

Eastham took out the lumbar drain. It had drained too much fluid, causing the brain, which usually floats in the cerebrospinal fluid, to settle down toward the brain stem, the way debris is sucked toward an emptying drain. The settling brain had hit the third cranial nerve, which regulates the pupils. A pupil "blowing" is the brain's canary in the mine. It means the brain, or part of the brain, is squeezing the brain stem. It often means the person is heading toward brain death.

Without the drain, Eastham had to find another way to relieve the pressure. So he removed the left part of Ryan's skull to allow more room for the brain to swell out and up, away from the stem.

During surgery, as Eastham cut the skull, a piece of bone cracked off near the original fracture line. The location of the broken piece was right above the sagittal sinus, the vein that empties blood from the brain. Perhaps the fracture had distorted the sagittal sinus, Eastham told me later, when he looked back on why Ryan's brain swelled so much. That would slow the drainage of

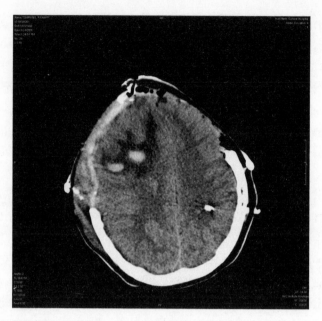

*CT scan of Ryan's head after his second craniectomy
shows where his skull has been removed.*

blood and aggravate the swelling. But there was no way to tell if
that's what was happening.

Eastham knew by then there wasn't a single cause to Ryan's
perplexing, life-threatening swelling. It was the overdrainage. It
was probably sagittal sinus thrombosis. It was probably the beginning of hydrocephalus, too, also known as water on the brain because the brain stops draining cerebrospinal fluid on its own. Each
condition is challenging enough by itself. Combine them and the
problems increase exponentially. After removing the bone flap,
Eastham inserted a drain through the back of the skull, deep into
the brain and into the left ventricle.

The rest of the day was a blur, one of those nightmares in
which you can't figure out where you are or what exactly is happening, only that some dark figure is bearing down on you and
your legs won't move and your mouth won't scream.

"He's stable," Barry said late in the afternoon. "Your parents
don't need to come out now."

Ryan was back in his room. Dr. Doom said the brain no longer was heading to the brain stem and that Ryan was in no imminent danger of dying, though he was still in critical condition.

I looked at Barry as if I had misunderstood him.

"What?"

Barry said I would be stressed by coordinating my parents' transportation and accommodations, and since Ryan was okay, they shouldn't come. Later I thought perhaps this was Barry's way of warding off ghosts. If my parents come out, then clearly Ryan is in danger. If they don't come, Ryan must be all right.

"I want them here," I said in a tone that made clear the subject was closed. "I need my mother."

My mother knew what it was like to lose a child.

At the age of thirty-three, my brother Bobby decided to have plastic surgery to fix the dent in his right temple, caused by a missing bone. During a routine blood workup, doctors found an abnormality, and X-rays revealed a tumor in his belly. He had malignant cancer in his intestines, stomach, pancreas, and liver. Surgeons took out as much as they could and told my parents there was no hope. No treatment could save him.

But in dying, Bobby came to life. He was weak and thin, yet he had never been happier. Suddenly everyone was rallying around him, paying attention. He was, for the first time, the center of attention, the recipient of cards and flowers. *Popular*. Rather than plunge him into a funk, dying lightened him. For the first time, he had problems that didn't draw taunts but rather sympathy and kindness. He was admired and fussed over.

But even in death, Bobby couldn't catch a break.

He had never touched drugs and only occasionally drank. Drinking and drugs didn't fit into his right-wing, judgmental, hippie-hating view of the world. After his surgery, however, Bobby popped painkillers like candy. He began washing them down with screwdrivers. He figured he was dying, so what did it matter.

Then just as suddenly as the cancer had appeared, it was gone.

Blood tests came up clean. The doctors had no explanation, given that Bobby had undergone neither chemotherapy nor radiation. My mother credited the bottle of holy water a friend had brought back from Lourdes. My mother had been adding it to my brother's food, praying that the drops from Lourdes, like baptismal water, had the power to cleanse and heal, allowing her son a new beginning.

Though the cancer seemed to be gone, Bobby had other problems: He had become addicted to the painkillers. He couldn't keep a job. He was drinking every night. One day my parents, with whom he had been living, received a call from the police in Cocoa Beach, two hundred miles away. Bobby had been picked up at a McDonald's. He had called 911 to report there were people in his car who would not get out. When police arrived, the car was empty. Witnesses said no one had gone near the car and that Bobby had been behaving irrationally. He was transported back to West Palm Beach and committed to a psychiatric hospital for observation. My parents had been trying to get help for him, but because Bobby was an adult, their hands were tied. Now, finally, his addiction could be addressed. Unfortunately, within twenty-four hours, the doctors concluded he was fine and let him go.

Things got so bad my parents kicked him out. It had been wrenching enough watching cancer almost kill him, they told Bobby, they'd be damned if they would sit around and watch him kill himself. He moved into a low-income apartment that soon smelled of vomit and old food.

He had been so ready to die he no longer could figure out how to live. He seemed to see this second shot at life not as a gift but as a betrayal. He was supposed to die. Dying was interesting and fulfilling in a way life had never been.

In the spring of his thirty-sixth year, Bobby learned his cancer had returned. He moved back in with my parents. As the disease swallowed him up, my mother sat with him every evening when she returned from her job as a secretary at the fire department. On the screened-in back patio, in the same blocky wooden chairs we sat in as children, my mother and brother talked for hours. She listened to his diatribes and ramblings but also to his childhood memories and stories about working with my father as a draftsman. She learned how to make him laugh. They had become friends.

I was still asleep when my mother called early one morning in 1995. When she told me Bobby had died, I cried. But when I hung up and began to get dressed, I suddenly had a vision of my brother. Not a vision, exactly. More of a glimpse. He was smiling in a way I had never seen. He seemed unburdened and free and energized, the way people look when they walk out of prison and take a deep breath of fresh air.

Fifteen

At Marin General, we stood in Ryan's ICU room with Eastham as he delivered instructions to the night nurse. He looked as exhausted as we were. Ryan was stable. He had come through. But we had had enough. We had gone through too many setbacks. Ryan couldn't afford any more.

That night, Barry and I took the phone into bed with us and called everyone we knew who could help us get Ryan transferred to UCSF immediately. By the time we went to sleep, it was all set: a pediatric ICU ambulance would pick Ryan up in the morning.

We went to sleep shaken but relieved that we were moving to a hospital that had a team of neurosurgeons, not just one, and an ICU that specialized in children.

The next morning, Friday, Ryan had a CT scan that showed the new drain was working well. The brain, Eastham said, was full but soft. The softness was a good sign; it meant there was no serious brain swelling. Ryan's ICP was in the teens. Eastham said he was going to ease up on the sedatives and cut back on the ventilator to start the process of waking Ryan from the coma.

Eastham's weeklong shift at Marin General—what he later said was the longest, most difficult week of his professional life—was over. He was feeling, as he later said, he "could rest on his oars." Things were stable. Ryan was leaving. Eastham was leaving.

"Where's the closest place to get a martini around here?" he asked, only half joking.

The critical care ambulance team from UCSF arrived around midday. They consulted with Ryan's nurses about his medications and history. Barry and I signed release forms. Eastham had just gotten off the phone with Dr. Nalin Gupta, a pediatric neurosurgeon at UCSF, to fill him in on Ryan's condition.

Then a nurse in Ryan's room called out to Eastham.

"His ICP is up," she said. "You better look at this."

Ryan's ICP had shot up to the 30s. Eastham pressed on Ryan's scalp. It was hard as muscle.

And Ryan's pupils were unequal—a harbinger of a blown pupil.

"There's no way," Eastham said. "This can't be happening."

He checked the drain. It had stopped working. He quickly adjusted the tube and got it going again. Ryan's ICP immediately dropped.

"We're okay," Eastham said.

The UCSF team rolled an enormous gurney into Ryan's room and began to set up the tubing, medicines, and ventilators.

But minutes later, Ryan's ICP shot up again. Eastham rushed back to Ryan's bedside. The drain was fine. But Ryan's brain was not only hard to the touch but much harder than it had been when Eastham had checked it just twenty minutes earlier.

"I don't believe this," Eastham said. "What is going on?"

He called Gupta at UCSF and explained what had just happened.

"I'm having trouble," Eastham said. "I can't figure out what's going on."

Eastham later said he didn't trust his own instincts or skills at that moment. How can this kid's intracranial pressure still be blasting up into the 30s nine days after his accident? It just doesn't happen. Eastham was questioning everything he had done. He went through it with Gupta step by step.

"My very best judgment is to not send him," Eastham told Gupta. "He's too unstable. Things are much worse."

Gupta agreed.

We had listened in mute horror to Eastham's conversation. We watched Eastham rush Ryan onto the elevator for his second CT scan of the day.

We watched the UCSF transfer team pack up their things and leave.

"I don't know how much more I can take," I said to Barry, crying again, huddled with him on the waiting room couch. Lorna had gone to pick my parents up from the airport shuttle bus.

Downstairs, Eastham scanned Ryan's brain and waited for the results. He had booked an OR. He guessed that Ryan's intracranial pressure had spun out of control during the night. Sometimes the pressure reaches a point and there's no pulling it back. The skyrocketing pressure could have shut down major blood vessels, disrupting circulation and causing strokes. Or the pressure could have caused more hemorrhaging, also triggering strokes. And the strokes could have killed off enough of the brain to cause irreparable damage. He imagined the scan would reveal a horror show— "nonsurvivable, really ugly stuff," he said.

He felt exhausted and defeated. What was it with this kid? Eastham couldn't believe that after wrestling the monster inside my son's head for a week, he was going to lose now. Later he told me it was the lowest point of his career.

When the scan was ready, Eastham called it up on the computer outside the OR.

"I need Tompkins," he barked at the technician, annoyed. "Where's Tompkins?"

"That *is* Tompkins," the technician said.

Eastham checked the name, time, and date on the scan.

"No way that scan is him," he said.

He flew back upstairs and bolted through the waiting room, summoning us to follow. "You're not going to believe this."

My parents had just stepped off the elevator. I hugged them, then Barry and I hurried to catch up with Eastham.

He called the scan up on the ICU computer.

"*Look* at that," he said. "It makes no sense."

Not only was there no evidence of strokes or new hemorrhaging, the midline shift had improved. Ryan's ventricles were more open than they had been in the morning scan; a slight fluid buildup was fixable with a second drain. Eastham went into Ryan's room and, at the bedside, drilled a tiny hole through the back of Ryan's skull. He inserted a second drain, this time into the right ventricle. Ryan's ICP immediately dropped to the low teens. His pupils had returned to normal. The brain felt soft again.

Eastham wouldn't let Ryan leave, however, until he had one more CT scan, his third of the day. He needed to be absolutely sure Ryan was stable. That CT scan looked even better than the last one.

"I can't explain it," he said when he returned to the ICU, where we had been waiting at Ryan's bedside.

Eastham knew my parents had just arrived from Florida.

"What time did they land?" he asked. I told him around two.

"That's about the time everything changed. It's as good an explanation as any."

I knew he was only partly serious, but I smiled to think about a doctor, especially one as hard-edged as Eastham, attributing any kind of healing to spiritual or supernatural causes.

Of course, I had not yet heard about my father's prayer.

My father and Ryan had become close in the years before the accident. Ryan thought my father was a riot. Where my father once barked at Ryan for breaking the rules of the house, now he teased and needled and delighted in Ryan's zingers in response. My father had mellowed as a grandfather. He was softer and more outwardly loving with Ryan than he had ever been with his own children. But maybe that was because Ryan was so loving with him.

Ryan ended every phone call to my parents with "I love you," and my parents responded in kind, though we had never been a family to utter those words to each other. Once, when the family had gathered in South Carolina for vacation, Ryan said something in the course of a conversation about not being my father's "real grandchild" because they didn't have the same blood.

My father pointed his finger at Ryan the way he once did with us when he was angry.

"You're my grandson like every other kid in this room, whether you like it or not," he said.

It was the perfect thing to say.

The night I had called from the hospital asking them to fly out, my father had said his usual prayers. Then he added one, choosing his words carefully.

"We're past the point of asking for help," he prayed. "That's not enough anymore. We're looking for a miracle. As sick as Bobby was, I never asked for it. If I have a miracle coming, I want it now."

It would be months before my father, as devout a Catholic as you'll find, accepted that his prayer was literally, concretely, stunningly answered. "You grow up Catholic and hear about miracles, and you pray for miracles, but you never think it's going to happen to you," he told me later.

Did I believe God saved Ryan in answer to my father's prayer? I believe that just as the pressure in Ryan's brain could rise high enough to kill him, the loving energy sent to Ryan from so many people was strong enough to save him.

And maybe my father's prayer, a few words in the dark, was the tipping point.

In the late afternoon, the ICU ambulance team, summoned back, drove Ryan to UCSF Children's Hospital.

We packed up all the food and cards we had accumulated over the nine days at Marin General. With my parents in the backseat, Barry and I drove across the Golden Gate Bridge and up Nineteenth Avenue to Judah to Parnassus. UCSF hospital sits like a hulking fortress at the top of Parnassus in one of the grayest, coldest spots in San Francisco. The building has no charm, no distinctive features, no hint of the colorful Haight–Ashbury neighborhood down the hill. But, I told myself as we pulled into the seven-level parking garage, we didn't need smiles and warmth. We needed the best doctors, nurses, and facilities the medical profession could offer.

In the sixth-floor pediatric ICU, a team of doctors was waiting, including one of the most well-respected neurosurgeons in the country, Dr. Geoff Manley. He was the chief of neurotrauma at San Francisco General, which works in collaboration with UCSF. Unbeknownst to us, he had been summoned by a mutual friend, the president of the San Francisco Giants, to look after us, even though Ryan would not be his actual patient.

Ryan's neurosurgeon was Dr. Gupta, a tall, soft-spoken man in his early forties. We watched the two men huddle with the ICU attending physician plus several interns, residents, and fellows. Behind them, in one of the ten glass-enclosed rooms inside the ICU, two nurses darted around Ryan's bed, arranging the mind-boggling paraphernalia: IV bags; monitors for his ICP, his two ventricular drains, and heart; urinary catheter; rectal tube; nasogastric tube; endotracheal tube; IV line in his clavicle, another in his right wrist.

UCSF also had arranged three daily shifts of nurse's aides, who the hospital referred to as sitters. They would sit at Ryan's bedside 24/7 so when he began coming out of his coma, he wouldn't pull at his tubes, pick at his stitches, or otherwise harm himself. Some brain trauma patients, especially ones who are as big and strong as Ryan, can hurl themselves out of bed.

Barry and I took all this in and knew we had made the right

decision to move Ryan. It was Friday night, nine days after the accident. We felt relieved and safe.

Eastham drove directly from Marin General Hospital to DiMaggio's restaurant in North Beach and drank martinis. (Ever the Red Sox fan, he later told me he likes DiMaggio's because it's named after a dead Yankee.)

Yet there he was Saturday morning at UCSF. I was dashing out of the UCSF lobby for coffee as he was barreling in, bleary-eyed and haggard but still crackling with energy. I threw my arms around him. I had never hugged him before. Maybe I felt like we were in this together, that we had survived a war and now the worst of the shelling was over. Eastham had come, on his day off, to check on Ryan. He wasn't ready to let go. (Neither was Jimette, Ryan's ICU nurse at Marin General. She called the ICU nurses at UCSF every day for two weeks.)

Later, Eastham came to believe that Ryan's consistent downward spiral during his nine days at Marin General could be traced to the sagittal sinus. He theorized that a jagged edge of the fracture had pressed on the vein and restricted the outbound flow of blood—an event called sagittal sinus thrombosis—thus explaining the accumulation of fluid and the recurrences of increased pressure. He speculated that the obstruction, for whatever reason, became critical on Friday morning, when Ryan's pressure shot up into the 30s, then began to disappear.

After Ryan's first full day at UCSF—a gorgeous Saturday in early September—my parents, Barry, and I had dinner with Lorna and Doug on their stone patio, surrounded by a terraced garden of roses and crepe myrtle. We drank wine and told jokes and laughed more than any of us could remember laughing. We weren't thinking about how we were *supposed* to act when someone you love is in ICU in a coma. We were beyond that.

And we were relieved that Ryan was at UCSF. We felt as if we could breathe again. We didn't know if Ryan was finally out of the woods, but it felt that way.

Now we were beginning to wonder: How much damage had there been? Who would our son be when he awoke? It was almost as if I was back at the moment when I saw the photo of Ryan's birth parents, months before he was born. I had constructed an image of this imaginary child. He would like books and sports. He would be cheerful and loving. He would be kind and respectful. Then I spent sixteen years cramming, shoving, and twisting Ryan to fit that mold, or at least some semblance of it.

Here I was again. Waiting for my child to show himself to me.

Sixteen

September 1, 2006

R yan!"
    I called his name several times. I had been holding his right hand and suddenly felt a slight squeeze. He was waking up. He had been at UCSF for a week.

"Ryan, sweetie, it's Mom. I've been missing you."

I felt another squeeze.

Barry had gone back to work, a decision he and I reached together. We needed the money, frankly; I had taken a leave of absence from the *Chronicle*. And because college football games are on Saturday, Barry could fly to a game on Friday and be home late Saturday night or early Sunday morning. He was home the rest of the week. I assured him that I would be fine; I had Lorna and our other wonderful friends to keep me company.

We were in Room 3 inside the sixth-floor pediatric ICU, or PICU. There were ten rooms, all glassed in, all made private by curtains and each family's respect for each other's pain. Between thirteen hundred and fourteen hundred children are admitted each year to UCSF's pediatric ICU. About half are transfers from other hospitals that are not as equipped to treat the devastating injuries and diseases that UCSF routinely handles.

At UCSF, doctors immediately began cutting back and readjusting the twelve medications Ryan had been on at Marin General: dopamine and phenylephrine to keep his blood pressure up; midazolam, Ativan, and propofol for sedation; fentanyl for pain; antibiotics Zosyn, fosphenytoin, and vancomycin (for pneumonia caused by the ventilator); diuretic Mannitol; stool softener Colace; and Protonix to prevent a bleeding ulcer.

The doctors had been worried that after nine days of treatment, including a bilateral craniectomy (which one UCSF neurosurgeon considered a "last-resort" procedure), Ryan's intracranial pressure was still in the 20s when he arrived. They feared the ICP was spiraling out of control. "In the spectrum of brain traumas, he's out there," one doctor conceded when I pushed him for a frank assessment.

But within forty-eight hours the pressure had dropped and stabilized in the mid- to high teens, and both drains into his skull had been removed. The hard cervical collar was swapped for a soft one. Ryan was on a bed pad that inflated and deflated every few minutes to prevent bedsores on his back and legs. A motor at the end of the bed regulated the air pressure. It worked beautifully—until the nurses discovered deep, black, weeping bedsores on Ryan's heels. At 6 feet 3, he was too long for the bed; his feet rested against the air-pressure motor—the contraption that was supposed to prevent pressure sores instead caused them. A specialist was summoned and even she winced at the sight of them. She said one was so deep that it likely would require surgery, which meant Ryan wouldn't be able to walk on it for at least three months.

I felt myself getting angry. Why wasn't it noticed? Ryan's rehab was going to be grueling and awful enough without having to contend with a painful, debilitating bedsore. But then I looked at what the nurses were handling: almost a dozen medications delivered in various tubes at precise times and doses, a ventilator, a Foley catheter to drain Ryan's bladder, a rectal tube, a nutrition bag, electronic monitors for ICP, heart rate, oxygenation. They had to stretch his arms and legs to prevent them from stiffening. They had to clean him and brush his teeth and change his sheets without disturbing all the tubes and wires. They were also dealing with Ryan's pneumonia, a common side effect of being on a ventilator. I later read that researchers found that the average patient in ICU requires 170 individual actions a day.

Okay. Move on.

It is what it is.

During that first week at UCSF, as Ryan was weaned from the sedatives with the help of methadone and Ativan, and freed from the ventilator, urinary catheter, and rectal tube, he had begun to move his left leg. The blow to the right side of his brain had paralyzed his left side. His ICP settled into the 10 to 13 range. He had scratched his nose several times with his right hand. Now, two weeks after the accident and a day after his breathing tube was removed, he was lightly squeezing my hand.

"Ryan, are you ready to wake up? Open your eyes, sweetie."

His eyelids parted. I was at his bedside by myself. Barry was in Los Angeles to broadcast a UCLA game.

"Ryan! Look at me."

Ryan turned his head toward my voice. His eyes opened. He looked at me, his gaze as cloudy as a newborn's. He seemed to be taking stock, not recognizing me yet as his mother. The last time he looked at me that way, in the nursery at Hemet Community Hospital, I was head-over-heels for him, but not yet in love. How could I be? He was as much a stranger to me as I was to him.

Now my heart broke open.

"I'm right here, baby-babe."

Ryan's face was impassive, completely frozen, either from the narcotics or the brain injury.

"Sweetie-pie, how are you feeling?"

His face and eyes gave me no clues to what might be going on inside his head. I couldn't tell if he was scared or happy or confused. I couldn't tell if he could understand what I was saying.

He raised his right hand as if trying to reach me. Now I was certain he recognized me. I took his palm and pressed it against my lips.

"You've been sleeping for a really long time."

He untangled his hand from mine and ran it over his head. His hair was shaved in the front and normal length in the back, making him look like Dr. Frankenstein's punk experiment. Ryan's fingers felt the strange railroad tracks of staples crisscrossing his scalp and the softness when he pressed down where his skull once had been. (Some compare the consistency of the brain to toothpaste, some to soft tofu. To me, at least the way it felt through the skin, it was more like a water balloon.)

Ryan couldn't sit up. He couldn't move his left arm or hand. He couldn't drink or eat. He wore a diaper.

I told him that he had fallen off his skateboard. That he was at UCSF in San Francisco. That Dad was in Los Angeles but would be back tomorrow. That he would be talking and moving around soon. That he would be fine.

Like a baby, he began exploring, reaching for everything in his sight: the IV in his arm, the nurse's hair, the bags of fluids on the metal pole by his bed.

The nurse gave him the suction wand to play with. It is similar to the one dentists use to clear out saliva. Ryan couldn't swallow, so thick, sticky gunk—it looked like white rubber cement—collected in his mouth and had to be suctioned out several times an hour.

Ryan waved the wand around, then stuck it in his ear. He pulled it out, then tried it again, exploring the strange suctioning sensation. Then he pressed it against his leg and face to see what that felt like.

"Ryan, touch the wand to your nose," I said, testing his comprehension.

He did. Then he stuck it up his nostril.

"Ryan," I said, laughing, "not *in* your nose!"

He pulled it out, then stuck it in his nostril again.

"Not *in* your nose!"

Then, of course, he did it again. He was doing it on purpose!
He was trying to be funny. That had to be a good sign.

Later in the day, when his right hand was grabbing restlessly
at the sheets and bed rail, I put a pen in his fingers and held a
notebook in front of him. He immediately began scribbling like
a toddler, scratches and scrawls all over the page. I asked him to
draw a circle. He drew a shaky, misshapen circle. I asked him to
draw a straight line. He did. Then a square. He understood! He
remembered! The ICU nurse was surprised his brain already could
direct his hand and that he could retrieve from his memory bank
what a circle and a square looked like.

When Barry called, I told him Ryan not only had woken up
but was following simple commands. I held the phone to Ryan's
ear. Ryan took the phone and held it himself, unable to speak but
craving the sound of his father's voice, the way he did when he
was a baby and Barry called from the road. He listened for only
a few seconds, though, dropping the phone and reaching for the
suction wand again.

Alone in bed that night, I was flipping through the TV chan-
nels and happened upon the Harrison Ford movie *Regarding Henry*.
Ford's character suffers a brain injury from a gunshot wound. He
doesn't recognize his wife or daughter. He has forgotten how to
tie his shoelaces. His tastes in food and clothing have changed
completely. He speaks like a slow-witted child.

I had to turn it off.

We had been warned that Ryan might not be the same child
we had raised for sixteen years. He was among the 5 percent of
brain injury patients whose trauma had been categorized as se-

vere. I knew from writing about soldiers wounded in Iraq that brain injury was the signature injury of the war, but I didn't know how common it was at home. Every year about sixty thousand Americans die from traumatic brain injuries, nearly twice as many as die from AIDS each year. Another seventy thousand to ninety thousand emerge with significant disabilities. According to the Centers for Disease Control and Prevention, 5.3 million Americans live with a disability resulting from TBI.

In one study I saw—months later, when I was able to read again—only 10 percent of children who had suffered severe brain injuries had normal neurological exams a year after their injury. Less than 30 percent had a normal IQ. About half had significant behavioral problems. Seventy-five percent needed special education services.

Most disturbing, brain trauma can scramble the circuitry so violently that it produces, in essence, a different person. Ryan's whole sense of self, of what makes him him, might have been smothered to death as his brain swelled inside the cramped confines of his skull.

I researched all this later. I didn't know any of it while I celebrated every tiny accomplishment in Ryan's ICU room, flaunting each one like an unearthed artifact. See? Everything's still here! He's going to be fine!

Lorna came by every day, and most days her daughter, Emma, came with her. She and Ryan were the same age but couldn't have been more different. Emma was a fast-talking, effervescent girl who loved fashion and played tennis and had a million friends. But, unlike Ryan, she was hesitant and even fearful of a lot of things, particularly unfamiliar situations. She and Ryan were as close as cousins.

In the ICU, Emma lingered in Ryan's doorway, reluctant even to look at her damaged friend. Lorna coaxed her one step closer with each visit. Ryan's eyes lit up when he caught a glimpse of her.

One night that first week at UCSF, the attending doctor, Scott Soifer, pulled Emma aside. He was a no-nonsense guy in his twenty-seventh year in the ICU.

"He's going to need your support," Dr. Soifer told Emma. "You don't know how far he's going to go. If you're a friend, you've got to be there for him. It's important to talk to him and treat him normally even when he can't talk back. You can't be afraid."

From that moment, Emma became Ryan's number 1 playmate. She could get him to try things no one else could. She set up a small hoop on the glass wall of the room and coaxed Ryan into throwing the NERF ball through it. She got Ryan to wave, form the peace symbol with his fingers, and toss a sock monkey that had become his favorite toy. (It seemed to be just the right size and softness. He clutched it to his chest when he fell asleep.)

We all racked our brains to keep him busy as he became more conscious and more restless. We gave him Play-Doh and his beloved Matchbox cars, squishy balls, and Slinkys. He wore a look that was alternately wide-eyed and blank. But Emma chatted away at him, as if he were one of her classmates. She shot disapproving looks at adults who talked to Ryan as if he were a baby, which was a temptation for all of us. He *was* so much like a baby.

Almost every moment of every day, from the time Ryan arrived at UCSF, we played Jack Johnson music through an iPod and a small set of speakers. Ryan paid little notice to the music or to anything else for very long. He couldn't yet focus on the television for more than a few seconds at a time. In response to questions, he could, at times, hold up one finger for yes. His focus was so fleeting that he couldn't manage to remember two fingers for no.

But every new gesture was evidence that Ryan's brain was rebooting, that a sentient being was inside. What we still could not know was how much would be him and how much would be some different boy, reconfigured, like a landscape, from the upheaval inside his head. So far he was funny and sweet and affectionate, like a baby who wanted nothing more than to be cuddled and stroked.

Ryan was improving at a pace that had doctors talking about releasing him from ICU within a week. He still had one tube draining excess fluid from his brain, and once that was removed, he could go to the regular pediatric ward.

One day, Lorna brought in a toy she thought Ryan would like. It was a plastic "grasper" usually used by people who can't bend to pick up things from the floor. With his right hand, he could squeeze the handle to make the claw at the end of the stick open and close. He tried to pinch our noses with it, though he usually missed; his eyes did not track well yet. The grasper made a grinding sound that perhaps gave Ryan some satisfaction, since he couldn't make noise on his own. He loved it.

Several days later, I arrived to find him slamming the grasper on the mattress. He couldn't tell me what was wrong, and his expressionless face gave no hint. I tried to distract him by putting a pencil in his hand. He stabbed the point into the paper, ripping it. He tossed the pencil across the room.

The ICU doctor said that Ryan might be starting to understand his situation. Nothing pleased him. Nothing soothed him. He tried to get out of bed by tossing his right foot over the railing. By this time, he was wearing heavy boots to protect the huge bedsores on each heel, and when he lolled his foot over the railing, the weight of the boot yanked his torso into the railing. The bed suddenly seemed to have become his prison. He couldn't get comfortable enough to sleep until he received Ativan to help him. Whenever the nurse injected the medication, it burned going into the vein, and Ryan thrashed around, trying to bite the poor woman. Other times, he closed his eyes and opened his mouth in a silent scream.

At one point, when Barry and I asked how we could help him, he pointed at his mouth, then cupped his hand and tilted it toward his mouth, as if drinking a glass of water. But he was not allowed to have water yet because he could not swallow. We gave him a wet sponge on a stick, then gave him a damp washcloth to bite on. Sometimes he threw it at us. We tried to interest him in the sock monkey and Play-Doh and photographs of family and friends. We held his hand and kissed his face and sang to him. He alternately hugged us and shoved us away.

We knew that anger was one of the stages of recovery for brain injuries, and in that way its appearance could be seen as progress. Still, it was wrenching to watch. It fed my fear that this could be who Ryan would always be, that even at this preposterously early point in his healing, the new Ryan had emerged and would never change back.

"How long can this stage last?" I asked one of the ICU doctors, a woman who looked to be eight or nine months pregnant. Barry and I were exhausted from trying, and repeatedly failing, to keep Ryan engaged and calm. We were drained from witnessing his misery. We needed reassurance.

"I know one patient who was like this for years," she said.

I stared at her. Did she have any idea how hateful that was? She cited the most extreme possibility and that was supposed to be helpful and informative?

I felt the same resentment toward the pediatric rehab doctor who visited Ryan one day in the ICU. She had read his charts and examined him. She stood at his bedside and told us that anyone with such a severe brain injury would have lifelong disabilities. They might be profound, she said, or they might not. But there would be something.

She couldn't know that yet, I thought. Was she trying to make sure we were "prepared"? That we should start thinking of our son as disabled now so that, if it happens, we will have gotten a jump on it? Wouldn't there be plenty of time to grieve and worry when and if the worst-case scenario actually came to pass? I told the ICU attending that I never wanted to see that rehab doctor again.

The next day, Ryan woke up more focused and alert and much calmer. When I wrote an R on a sheet of paper, he wrote a shaky but clear R underneath. Throughout the morning, he fixed his eyes on the television for several minutes at a time—another first. When Barry arrived in Ryan's room after three days in LA, Ryan stretched his right arm toward him. His face still couldn't show emotion, but his eyes lit up. Barry bent to kiss him and Ryan laid his arm across Barry's back, the best hug he could manage. He patted Barry's back, then stroked his face.

"Just leave my honker alone," Barry said. Barry's prominent nose has always been fodder for jokes between them.

Ryan grasped Barry's nose between two bent fingers and shook it. Barry laughed.

"If Dad stays bent over you like that for too much longer, you're going to have to give him one of your famous back massages," I said.

Ryan immediately switched from patting Barry's back to scratching it.

Late in the afternoon, Ryan showed Barry the pen his sister Andi, Barry's older daughter, had given him that morning. When Ryan clicked the top, out came the very proper British voice of baby Stewie from the cartoon *Family Guy*.

"I come bearing a gift," Stewie said. "It's in my diaper, and it's not a toaster."

Barry did a dead-on imitation. For the first time, the right corner of Ryan's mouth turned up. He was smiling. His left side was still paralyzed, so the smile was weak and lopsided but thrilling enough to turn Barry and me into Catskills comics to get him to do it again. I told him that with all the gunk in his throat—he still was too weak to cough—his breathing sounded like Darth Vader.

"I am your fah-tha," I said, dropping my voice an octave.

Ryan tried to mimic the words, parting his lips, but no sound would come. I joked that Dad and I would look back on this period of muteness with wistful longing. The rest of the day, Ryan kept moving his mouth, itching to talk. Barry joked and laughed, as he had always done with Ryan. Sometimes they seemed more like buddies than father and son. I watched how Ryan's eyes followed him around the room. But I also noticed his eyes searching for me. Once when Barry was standing at the side of the bed, Ryan turned to me and held his arm out. He pulled me close and pressed his lips to my face, unable to pucker for a proper kiss.

"I love you, sweetie-pie," I said.

When we left for the night, Barry kissed Ryan a dozen times on his cheeks and forehead and told him we'd be back in the morning. As Barry gathered the newspapers and cell phones, I bent and kissed Ryan and told him that I loved him, then laid my cheek against his. I felt his dry lips on my ear. And I heard his first word: light, raspy, barely audible.

"Mom."

His first word as a baby had been "ball."

Now, "Mom."

My throat went dry. I blinked back tears. My love for him gripped me like a physical force. This 6-foot-3-inch Ryan was as sweet and helpless and amazing as that tiny creature who once slept under a mobile of yellow ducks: he could not yet speak, walk, eat solid food, or use a bathroom; he needed tons of sleep.

I thought about the theory that we are all ages at once. When we are forty-five, we are also, somewhere inside, the selves we were at five and twenty and thirty-two. It occurred to me that the baby inside my sixteen-year-old son had reemerged. I was back in the rental car in Hemet, driving away from Tony and Seyth and the maternity ward, staring down at this amazing creature in his car seat.

That baby was with me now.

And he was giving me a second chance.

Seventeen

It was September 7, twenty-four days after the accident and about two weeks into the fall semester of what should have been Ryan's sophomore year of high school. A CT scan showed what we already knew from the bulges that had developed under Ryan's scalp: both ventricles had refilled. And he had developed an infection. They would treat it with broad-spectrum antibiotics while they waited for the results of the bacteria culture.

We were beginning to understand how different the rhythm of illness was from the rhythm of life, especially now that the adrenaline of the first few weeks had disappeared. Even though everyone told us it would be up and down and all over the place, something in our own brains kept expecting a straight path. But hospitals, or maybe illness, are so much about letting go of everything you think you know and giving yourself over to a pace and direction that are completely out of your hands, no matter how much you study, or how many good questions you ask, or how much time you spend at the bedside doing all the things a caring parent is supposed to do.

It felt a little like walking the labyrinth at Grace Cathedral in San Francisco. The circuitous path of twists and turns eventually leads to the center. It's supposed to remind you that just when you think you are heading straight for your destination, your path takes a turn, leading you farther away. But you go with it and end up where you are supposed to end up.

After the excitement of Ryan's awakening and first word, he spent several days asleep. Then we arrived the morning of September 9, a Saturday, to find Ryan playing "rock, paper, scissors" with a nurse's aide.

"Ry! That's unbelievable!" I said. "Look at you!"

The nurse said he had been awake most of the night, as alert as she had seen him since he arrived at UCSF.

We called in the ICU doctor.

"Do you see what he's doing?" Barry said.

We wanted to make sure the doctor saw this with his own eyes.

"Ryan," the doctor said in a loud voice. "Hold up two fingers."

Nothing. Ryan grabbed for the suction wand.

"Ryan!" the doctor repeated. "Hold up two fingers!"

Ryan held up two fingers.

The doctor tapped his right hand. "Raise this hand. Ryan! Raise your right hand!"

Ryan's eyes wandered back to the doctor. He raised his right hand.

"Raise this hand," the doctor said, tapping the left.

Nothing. The left arm and hand were still paralyzed.

Instead, Ryan lifted his right hand again.

"The *left* hand, Ryan," the doctor said.

Ryan reached over with his right hand, grabbed the left, and lifted it.

We cracked up. Even the usually stone-faced doctor laughed.

"Okay, great," he said. "He's got a sense of humor."

Barry and I beamed as if our son had just explained Fermat's Last Theorem.

That afternoon, the nurses slid Ryan into a neurochair, a huge contraption that starts as a flat bed, then with the touch of a few buttons, reconfigures itself into a chair. It's for patients who cannot sit up on their own. To protect his head, Ryan had to wear a special helmet made of foam rubber the color of Yoo-hoo. He looked as if he belonged in the backfield of a 1920s football team. (So there was your irony: because he didn't wear a helmet for ten seconds, he would have to wear a really ugly one for months, until his bone flaps were reattached.)

We wheeled Ryan to the door of his room so he could see what was beyond it. His eyes opened wide as he took in the hub of the pediatric ICU. There were desks, chairs, and monitors with nurses and doctors walking in and out of glass-enclosed rooms. Ryan's facial muscles still couldn't move, so we couldn't tell if he was shocked, confused, or frightened by where he was. We told him yet again that he had had a skateboarding accident and that he was in the hospital in San Francisco. I held his hand and told him he was going to be fine, that these doctors and nurses had taken care of a lot of kids like him. I didn't know if he understood any of it. He began banging his booted foot. He seemed on the verge of tears.

When we returned him to bed, he reached for me with his right hand. I stood at the right side of the bed and bent over him so he could give me a hug. He laid his arm across my back. When I began to rise, he held me tighter. I nuzzled my face into his neck. I kissed him on the cheek. He turned his head and kissed me back. I stayed that way, bent at the waist, my head on his chest, until he fell asleep.

He craved affection every waking minute. He wanted just to hold Barry and me, and also Lorna and other close friends and family who came to visit. Everyone had to give him a hug and accept a kiss, which was completely out of character for Ryan. He was always a hugger but never a kisser, not even with Barry and me. We would bombard him with kisses and he rarely reciprocated. We knew he was truly sorry or wildly appreciative of something when he planted a kiss on our cheeks. It did not come naturally. Now he insisted on kisses, opening his right arm and inviting visitors into his embrace so he could press his lips to their faces.

I found myself, in response, stroking him and kissing him and practically crawling into bed with him. Only the spiderweb of tubes and wires prevented me. I couldn't get enough of him. It was as if a latch had been sprung on a box, and everything soft and vulnerable inside me gushed out. His breath had this rancid odor, which is typical of people in comas. Mucus and saliva sit so long in the mouth and throat that they ferment and rot. Yet when I was driving home from the hospital and getting into bed at night, I sought out the smell on my hands and clothes. It reminded me of him.

Eighteen

On Monday afternoon, September 11, I wrote Yes and No on a pad of paper and asked Ryan to point to one or the other in answer to questions.

"Do you know where you are?" I asked.

He didn't point but instead took the pen and wrote his own yes, then wrote another word I couldn't decipher. It started with a Z, but neither Barry nor I could make out the rest of the scribble.

"Write it again, Ryan."

He wrote it again, just as garbled.

"I don't know what it is, Ry. Write it slower."

Again he wrote the same scribble.

"Sorry, Ryan. I still can't read it."

Then he wrote, "You ar stup . . ."

Before he finished, I said, "You are stupid?"

Barry and I burst out laughing. Ryan laughed, too, in the weird way he came to do, with a half-cocked smile and the slightest guttural sound.

On the way back from lunch, encouraged by Ryan's attempts to write, Barry and I stopped at a hardware store and bought a white erasable board. We propped it on Ryan's lap. I wrote, "I love you," wondering if he might mimic me. He took the pen and wrote what looked like "Mom."

"'Mom'?" I asked. "Raise one finger if that's a yes."

He did nothing. We erased "Mom." Then Ryan wrote, in more legible letters, "I love you."

"Great, Ry!" I said. "I love you, too."

With painstaking effort, he continued: "but you are a pain in the butt."

Barry and I howled. We noticed that even with an injured brain, he spelled both but(t)s correctly.

In the afternoon, Barry, Ryan, and a sitter named Tonya were watching a classic car show on television, and an old Corvette appeared on the screen.

"Oh, that's a '57," Tonya said. She said her brother owned one.

Ryan raised his right hand and flashed five fingers twice: 1955. He was right.

"What was the first year for Corvettes?" Barry asked.

Ryan flashed five fingers, then four: 1954. Right again.

His brain was working.

In late afternoon, the neurosurgeon, Dr. Gupta, came by. In med school, he had made the unusual decision to specialize in pediatric neurosurgery. The American Society of Pediatric Neurosurgeons has only one hundred or so members, about a dozen of whom practice outside the United States. Half of the twelve to eighteen fellowships offered around the country in the subspecialty go unfilled each year. Yet more than a million children sustain traumatic brain injuries every year in the United States. Twenty thousand are permanently disabled. About ten thousand die. I was particularly struck by this statistic: 43 percent of all deaths among five- to nine-year-olds are from traumatic brain injuries.

Gupta showed us the CT scan from the day before. The buildup of fluid on the left side of Ryan's brain had grown slightly larger compared to the CT scan taken a few days earlier. Gupta said he was going to extract the fluid—a fairly straightforward bedside procedure—and watch for the next forty-eight hours to see if it returned or if the brain was able to absorb it.

If there was a substantial buildup, he said, he would have to put in a shunt, though he hoped he wouldn't have to. A shunt is a thin tube that carries fluid from the brain and empties it into the abdominal cavity. But if the fluid didn't return, or if it built up slowly, Gupta said he would consider releasing Ryan directly to a rehab facility later in the week and keeping an eye on the fluid through periodic CT scans.

We discovered that Kentfield Rehab Hospital, about a half-mile from our house, had a top-rated brain injury program. We knew the facility fairly well. Barry's mother had been at Kentfield twice for lung problems, and Barry's father once after a stroke. I had positive feelings about the place because of their experiences. The first image that came to mind, though, when I thought of Kentfield Rehab was the oak tree.

The oak rose from the middle of the hospital's upper lot, just a few yards from the bike path where I walked Bill the dog almost every morning. Its trunk was as big around as a garage. Its branches were heavy and thick enough to be trees in their own right. To me, the majestic tree made the plain, squat hospital seem grand and solid.

I thought about being close enough to walk to the hospital every day. Friends from Ross could visit so easily. Bill could stop by during his walk every morning. We went home that night trying to keep ourselves from thinking too much about Ryan moving closer to home. We didn't want to get our hopes up. We had done that too much already.

Sure enough, Ryan plunged again into a dark wretched misery the next day, Tuesday. He thrashed in his bed. Pushed us away. Threw the sock monkey at the door. Yanked at his sheets. Kicked the bed rail. He pounded us on the back or pushed us away. His legs and head flopped all over the place. He grew particularly agitated when we moved him to the neurochair. When I gave him the erasable board to see if he could tell us the trouble, he stabbed the marker onto the board, flattening the marker's nub.

"What is it, Ryan? Do you need cream for your head? Does it itch? Your foot? Point to what's bothering you."

He pointed at his mouth. He cupped his hand and tilted it toward his lips. Water was the one thing he craved, and I couldn't give it to him.

"No water yet, Ry," I said. I wanted to pour a pitcher of it into his mouth. "Soon."

The ICU doctor said Ryan would be starting physical therapy now that he was awake. We hoped the exertion—and possibly a change of scenery if he went to the physical therapy room— would release some of the agitation and pent-up energy.

The doctors told us early on that we had to take this journey day by day, and sometimes hour by hour. But we realized they were bracing us not only for the length of the recovery but the tumult and changeability of it. We never knew from one day to the next which Ryan we would get. We enjoyed the good days and accepted the bad ones. I wrote in my notebook, "You don't need to go to a monastery in Tibet to learn about living in the moment. Just spend a month in an ICU."

But Tuesday morning, just twelve hours after I committed those Zen-ish words to paper, I cracked.

Here was a kid who, even before the brain injury, couldn't sit through dinner and now he had been in bed for almost a month. He needed to move his body, get out of bed, see something other than the glass partitions of Room 3 in the PICU.

"Can we get the neurochair?" I asked our nurse. "Ryan needs to sit up."

I had been expecting the physical therapist to develop a schedule for Ryan now that everything except his left hand was working.

"We don't know where it is," she said.

"Can someone go find it?"

She explained that the chair belonged to the neuro unit on the seventh floor. The nurses up there weren't sure where it was. Ryan was banging the claw on the mattress and slamming his boot against the rail.

"Really, is this too much to ask? I mean how hard can it be to find it?"

"I'm not sure there's anyone available."

"How about I go up there?" I said, trying to keep the anger and frustration out of my voice.

"It doesn't work like that."

I finally exploded. I was like Al Pacino in *Dog Day Afternoon*. I demanded to see all of Ryan's records. I wanted to know why no one was *doing* anything. Where was a schedule of therapies and a list of goals and objectives for my son's rehabilitation? Did I have to do it all myself?

Ryan was still in ICU, of course, barely able to focus on anything for more than a few seconds, a detail that had no impact on me whatsoever. I stopped just short of clapping my hands and barking, "Let's *go*, people!" My issues with control, dormant for the most part since the accident, lunged out, snarling and drooling, like something out of *Alien*.

An ICU doctor was summoned.

"You can't look at the records without someone from the hospital to explain it," he said gently.

"They're my son's records! I have every right to see them whenever I want!"

I didn't know if I did or not. I just wanted information. Information made me feel as if I was *doing* something. The ICU doctor brought out a huge binder and began to go through it. I took notes furiously, though I had little idea what I was writing. At least, I felt, I was putting them all on notice that I was Paying Attention. In reality, I was making a fool of myself.

I knew, of course, that UCSF was doing an excellent job medically. But the communication in such a huge hospital is less than perfect. We found out second and third hand that Ryan likely would not be leaving ICU or going to Kentfield Rehab until the following week. The spot on his head that had been drained the previous night had refilled with fluid within hours, so doctors had to figure out why, and whether Ryan would require a shunt. Until then, Ryan was stuck in ICU. The accumulation of fluid on his brain apparently was affecting his coordination. He couldn't make any of his writing legible and finally tossed the erasable board off the bed.

Then he got even worse, and it was my own fault. His new sitter had asked what had happened to Ryan. We were standing by Ryan's bed. I said he had fallen off a skateboard, had two surgeries to remove parts of his skull, two drains, and had been in ICU for a month. I don't know what I was thinking, saying it in front of Ryan.

He clearly comprehended what I had said. His face contorted in raw grief and anguish. He couldn't produce tears, which made the whole thing even more wrenching. He turned away from me, burying his face into a pillow that had been propped against the side railing. I tried to recover by telling Ryan that lots of kids have had the same kind of accident and that he'd be fine just as they were and that it would just take a little time. But he was in a funk for the next few hours.

Later, when Ryan finally was in the elusive neurochair, he kept trying to pull off his helmet, seeming to be irritated by the way it felt on his head. Then he began pointing at his right shin and foot and again contorted his face. We asked if he was in pain. Thumbs up. But no one could figure out the source. So we asked the nurse to give him Tylenol. There was nothing else to do.

That evening, Dr. Manley, the neurosurgeon from San Francisco General, stopped by. Ryan immediately stuck out his hand to shake the doctor's hand. Dr. Manley couldn't believe how well

Ryan was doing, despite his agitation. I asked him how we could get Ryan started on occupational therapy (OT), physical therapy (PT), and speech therapy.

"Nothing's happening," I complained. "There's no routine. No plan that I can tell. I can't get anyone to do anything."

"He's still in ICU," Dr. Manley said. "He's not ready for therapy yet. The best rehab right now is exactly what you're doing. Your interaction with Ryan is the best thing for him. Just be there with him."

We didn't need every expert we could get our hands on.

We were enough.

Nineteen

The next morning, Wednesday, apparently in response to my nut-job tirade, the nurse not only had tracked down a neurochair, Ryan was already sitting in it when we arrived. His trunk muscles had gotten strong so quickly. He had begun to pull himself up to a sitting position, his back supported by pillows. Through the day, every specialist in the hospital seemed to make a pilgrimage to Ryan's room. We had occupational therapy and physical therapy. We had the speech therapist and the social worker. We had the Child Life Department (which tends to the child's social and educational needs) and the infectious disease doctor. We had the neurosurgeon and the attending ICU doc. We were about to start handing out numbers like at a deli counter.

That day, September 13, almost a month after the accident, Ryan stood for the first time. The OT and PT worked both sides of the bed to get Ryan to sit up with his legs over the edge of the mattress. They positioned his feet on the floor, gently adjusting his trunk and shoulders for balance. With his arm looped around Barry's shoulder, Ryan stood. I snapped a photo.

The triumph lasted only a second, however. Ryan's face twisted in pain, and he sank back down on the bed.

The neurosurgeon, Dr. Gupta, stopped by to tell us that he wasn't worried about the fluid around Ryan's brain. It was pooled between the brain and the scalp; when it was time to open the scalp in order to replace the bone flaps, the fluid would drain out. And it would not reaccumulate because the reattached bones would force it to be reabsorbed or excreted.

Gupta also answered a question I had been asking since leaving Marin General: Where were the pieces of Ryan's skull? Nobody seemed to have a definite answer. They were stored somewhere, waiting to be retrieved when Ryan was ready to have them reattached. Some doctors store the bone in the patient's abdomen to decrease the risk of infection. Dr. Eastham didn't do that, but he wasn't sure where Marin General had stored Ryan's flaps. I knew they weren't lost, so I wasn't particularly worried. But I needed someone to give me an actual location. Gupta announced he had tracked the skull bones to an Oakland tissue bank that has a contract with Marin General. One less thing to worry about.

If the infectious disease doctors felt that the infection (we were never clear if it was staph or meningitis) was under control, Gupta said, Ryan likely would be released from ICU by the end of the day.

As we waited to find out if and when Ryan would move, Jennifer, the speech therapist, gave him a swallow test. She fed him a small piece of ice on a plastic spoon. He crunched down on it and swallowed.

"Good," Jennifer said, touching Ryan's throat with two fingers to feel the swallow.

She tried ice twice more, successfully, then fed him a half-teaspoon of water. It slid down his throat too quickly for his brain to send it down the right passageway. It went into his lungs instead of his stomach, and he coughed. So Jennifer gave him something called thick water, which is the consistency of honey and is flavored with lemon.

Ryan took the half-teaspoon and twisted his face as if he had just tasted a raw lemon. He took the washcloth I happened to be holding and wiped his tongue. Jennifer tried one more time with the thick water, and again Ryan recoiled. Then he bent over, pulled me down toward him, and put my hand on his stomach.

"Your stomach hurts?" I asked. He nodded.

We returned to moist sponges on a stick, a poor substitute for the elemental pleasure of water.

At seven that night, Ryan was released from ICU.

We walked next to the gurney as attendants wheeled him onto the elevator and up to the seventh floor. I had visited the seventh floor several nights earlier to scope out where Ryan might land. Or rather I intended to visit the floor, which I knew to be mostly kids with cancer. I had pushed the round metal button that opens the double doors and had barely taken two steps inside when I saw a family crying softly near the nurses' station. There were maybe four or five of them huddled so tight that you could barely tell where one person ended and another began. Their shoulders heaved. I didn't want their grief anywhere near me. I walked back out.

Now we passed rooms with cribs and quiet babies and mothers who looked up from their bedside chairs as Ryan's gurney squeaked past their doors. I wondered what horrors had visited these rooms. But we, at least, were okay now. The worst was over. We were out of ICU. It meant we soon would be packing up Ryan's iPod and Matchbox cars and going to rehab.

Twenty

The new room looked out onto a flat roof with huge pipes connected at right angles like a jungle gym. It was industrial and utilitarian. Sometimes we could catch a glimpse of trees or rows of Monopoly houses rising and falling along the hills of western San Francisco. Mostly, though, we saw fog. Pipes and fog. There was something safe about them, something that said this was a place that meant business.

Unlike ICU, where most families stayed inside their glass-enclosed rooms, the seventh floor sometimes felt like the freeway at rush hour. A mother holding her sick baby on her lap made her way down the hall in a wheelchair. The baby was connected by plastic tubes to a tree of IVs pushed by a nurse walking a few steps ahead. There was a boy of about seven in a wheelchair moving in the opposite direction. I had seen him before. He always had a surgical mask over his face. His mother pushed his chair. And on it went. Sick children and resilient parents, or at least parents putting up good fronts.

We still had twenty-four-hour-a-day sitters provided by the hospital. Even with the sitters, though, we could not get a clear picture about what was keeping Ryan awake at night. He needed lots of sleep to heal, but he was so easily stimulated. The hospital already had moved him from a room near the noisy nurses' station to one down the hall.

The big life-threatening problems were over, but in their place crept what seemed like a thousand smaller ones that wore us down bit by bit.

The worst was the IV.

Ryan had been poked so often that his body seemed to be in revolt, somehow wrangling the IV lines out of his veins nearly as fast as the nurses could put them in. Each new needle, pressed into flesh already bruised and sore from previous IVs, sent Ryan into spasms of writhing, violent pain. Often the medication burned as it entered his bloodstream. Extra nurses had to be summoned to hold him down.

Barry and I had learned over that first month that there were times when we did not need to bear witness to our son's misery. Our presence did not help him when they were poking him with sharp objects, so we left. We would go down to the cafeteria to get another coffee, or sit in the waiting room and stare at the angelfish in the aquarium. We stopped trying to fix Ryan's every discomfort because there was no fixing so much of it. The restlessness and frustration just were. The pain just was. We couldn't prevent it. Being a journalist, I think, helped me rationalize this, which is another way of saying I could distance myself when I needed to. At least some of the time.

We were relieved late on that first day on the seventh floor to discover there was a solution to Ryan's IV torture: a peripherally inserted central catheter. The PICC line is a thin tube inserted into a large vein in the arm. The tube is then snaked up to a main vein near the heart. The line is sutured to the arm to keep it in place. It serves as a universal port: all IV meds can be delivered through the PICC line, which can remain in place for months.

But the IV was only a piece of Ryan's misery. His feet hurt from the bedsore boots, not to mention the bedsores themselves. He had virulent diarrhea. His bottom hurt from a raw, red rash. Even applying a cooling balm triggered cries and kicks and flailing punches. Most worrisome was a sore on the front of his scalp at the juncture of the two craniectomies.

It was triangular, about the size of a dime and covered by a crusty scab. Beneath the wound was the thin covering of Ryan's brain. The scab was the only thing standing between Ryan's brain and the germs and bacteria swirling through the air. If the scab came off, his brain would be at high risk for infection.

Of course, Ryan couldn't help picking at it. Every few seconds, it seemed, Ryan's hand reached up and yanked off the bandage, prompting everyone in the room to leap at him and cry, "No!" He knew he wasn't supposed to touch the bandage. He clearly didn't want to touch it. But his hand impulsively went there, and before any of us could grab his arm, the bandage was off.

Almost nothing in those first days on the seventh floor could make him comfortable, much less happy. Ryan especially didn't seem to want me around. Without words, he asked me to leave several times, pointing to me, then to the door. I didn't take it personally. I wasn't offended or defensive. I didn't take it, as I did when he was a baby, as rejection. I knew this was about Ryan's discomfort and confusion, not about his feelings for me.

No sooner would Ryan order me from the room than his aide would come fetch me in the waiting room or call me on my cell. She would say he was saying Mom, and when she asked if he wanted Mom, he gave the thumbs up. I would go back only to be pushed away again. He beat up on Barry, too, hugging him, then shoving him away, smacking him on the arms and torso. He always seemed to follow the outbursts at both of us with long hugs and kisses all over our faces.

In his restlessness one day, Ryan kept reaching for a blue vinyl chair near his bed. He seemed desperate to sit in it. The physical therapist, with careful maneuvering, guided him from the edge of the bed into a standing position, then into the chair. The effort exhausted Ryan. He wanted immediately to get back into bed. He looked as if he might throw up. Maybe he was light-headed. His legs, which had always been like tree trunks, were bony and soft, like a sick old man's. Ryan had weighed about 220 pounds at the time of the accident. I was guessing he wasn't even 170 now.

Depending on which nurse or doctor we spoke with, Ryan's in-fection was either staph infection or meningitis. He either would end his antibiotic cycle on Monday or late the following week. He either would be ready to go to Kentfield Rehab over the weekend or sometime next week.

After a while, you stopped listening. Things would happen when they happened.

In those first few days out of ICU, Ryan was beginning to talk more. He sounded like someone with severe, whispery laryngitis rather than, say, a garbled stroke victim. Bit by bit, he was making himself understood. We were watching the sitcom *Malcolm in the Middle*, and a flock of bats flew from a cabinet. Ryan knew I had a bat phobia.

"That would be my worst nightmare," I said.

Ryan smiled his one-sided Elvis smile.

"It . . . would . . . be . . . funny," he rasped.

When the nurse asked one morning if he was in pain—part of the routine check-in at the start of every shift—Ryan shook his head.

"Un . . . com . . . fort . . . a . . . ble."

It made me chuckle. Five tortured syllables when "kind of" would have sufficed. It was the sort of precise word choice that had always taken me by surprise.

I went to dinner at Rob and Erin Becker's house one night when Barry was out of town. I had fallen into a schedule of going to Chris and Eric Lindner's on Monday nights and the Beckers' on Wednesdays. I ate with Lorna almost every other night.

Before dinner, Rob and Erin's son Cal, a few years younger than Ryan, said grace. I bowed my head, happy for the conversation and food and the normalcy of a family dinner.

". . . and God bless Ryan," Cal concluded.

Suddenly I was crying. God bless Ryan. Oh my God. Ryan's not here. He's in the hospital. He's hurt so bad he can't be with us. Why did it hit me right then? I felt sick and sad and wondered how I had managed to keep myself in denial day after day. I guess it was a skill I had honed all of my life—a practiced ability to protect myself. I hated what I felt right then, such fear and grief. What if Ryan never walked? What if he could never return to school or live on his own? I pushed the thoughts away. Enough. Get a grip. Giving in to fear and speculation was self-indulgent and weak. I wiped my tears and asked Erin to pass the mashed potatoes.

Twenty-one

The doctor I never wanted to see again walked through Ryan's door on a Friday afternoon, two days after he had moved out of ICU. She was the pediatric rehab doctor who had told me, as Ryan was just emerging from his coma, that such a severe head injury would mean permanent disability. I had hated her certitude. I felt, as ridiculous as it was, that she was dangerous, someone I had to keep away from my son, as if her predictions of doom could affect the actual course of his recovery.

She said she was there to do a quick evaluation. She held a pen in front of Ryan.

"Ryan, what is this?"

"A pen," Ryan said in his marble-mouthed, raspy, obscene-phone-call voice. She asked a series of simple questions that he answered correctly. Then she asked if he knew why he was in the hospital.

Ryan gave a half smile.

"Because I'm stupid."

The words were so garbled I had to translate. The doctor laughed.

He knew exactly what he had done: skateboarded without a helmet. I wasn't sure until that moment that he had understood that.

"What happened?" the doctor asked.

"I fell."

She asked him how an apple and an orange are similar. Most people apparently say they are fruit or they are round.

"They both taste good," Ryan said.

The doctor laughed again. "Perfect answer! Ryan, I'm very proud of you. You're doing a great job."

Then she and I stepped out in the hallway.

"I'm incredibly impressed," she said. She seemed genuinely pleased and surprised. "It was not just his answers but how long he was able to pay attention." She said the healthy tissue in his brain was taking over for the damaged tissue.

After so many long faces and pitying tones from nurses, doctors, and specialists, her words were validating. Barry and I had never doubted how this story would play out, or almost never doubted. We were just waiting for everyone else at the hospital to catch up.

Soon after she left, the phone in Ryan's room rang. Before I could reach it, Ryan picked it up. He babbled into it like a baby, his words incomprehensible. It was our friend Mickey, who was nonetheless thrilled that Ryan was alert and making sounds. When we hung up, I asked Ryan if he wanted to try talking to Grandma and Grandpa. Thumbs up.

"I have someone who wants to say hello," I said when my father picked up.

Ryan put the phone to his ear.

"Ahgamba," he said.

My father couldn't understand what he said. But I did. *Hi, Grandpa.* My eyes filled. I felt the way I did when Ryan was a baby babbling into the phone and I was interpreting, proud of his mastery of words that no one else could understand.

Later that day, more good news. The Kentfield Rehab admissions person said Ryan probably could be moved on Tuesday, four days away. When we told Ryan that evening, he gave a thumbs up. But did he know what it meant to move to rehab? Would it be difficult for him to be just blocks from our home but unable to go there yet?

The next day, Barry and I were hanging out in his room before dinner. I was making a to-do list. *Make appointment to meet doctor at Kentfield Rehab. Call* Chronicle *about family leave pay. Return iPod speakers to Pillsburys. Call back Mickey and Norma.* My game face had begun to return. There was work to be done now that Ryan was heading into the rehab phase.

I added to my list: *Three-ring binders. Brain injury research/ books.*

All the day's visitors had gone home. Ryan noticed that someone had left a bottle of water on the windowsill. He asked for it by pouring an imaginary drink into his mouth.

"Ryan, you know you can't have water yet," I said, forever the enforcer, the follower of the rules. He could get pneumonia if the water went into his lungs.

Ryan slapped the mattress.

"It's for your own good, sweetie," I said, the standard response to anything unpleasant I had required Ryan to do during the past sixteen years. It had been a polite way of saying, "Buck up. This is the way it is. Get over it."

Barry gave Ryan a green sponge on a stick. After about four of them, Ryan pointed to the bottle on the windowsill.

"Real water," he whispered. His eyes locked on mine.

I'm not sure why I did what I did next. I didn't think about it. There was no conscious decision, no internal debate. I rose from my chair, walked to the windowsill, and picked up the bottle. I filled the bottle's tiny cap about halfway—maybe a teaspoon's worth. I told Ryan to sit up straight and to tuck his chin as he swallowed, the way the speech therapist had been teaching him.

I emptied the cap into his mouth. He tucked and swallowed.
"More," he said.

I poured water from the cap three more times. Barry shot me a look. I ignored him. Ryan was swallowing well, and he coughed only once, and very gently.

Thirty minutes later, he leaned over the railing of the bed and spit the water back up.

That night, Ryan fell asleep on his side, curled up, with a deflating Sponge Bob balloon between his knees. I had stayed at the hospital because Ryan had not been sleeping well. When he awoke at 10:30, a nurse had just come in. She was on the other side of the bed from me, unfurling a cuff to take his blood pressure.

Ryan asked her for water.

She launched into the spiel he heard every time he asked: the speech therapist hadn't approved it yet, he could get pneumonia, she would give him a damp sponge on a stick.

Ryan turned and looked up at me the way he did as a baby in his crib, his eyes big and soft, taking me in as if I were an amazing dream, a miracle come true right in his room.

"Mom, " he sighed. "The water giver."

I felt tears on my face before I fully comprehended what he said. I suddenly saw what he saw at that moment: a nurturer, a soother, a comforter.

I was the mother he had been waiting for, the one who finally found her way to him.

The water giver.

I let the words wash over me.

They felt like absolution.

Twenty-two

It was another football Saturday, September 16. Barry was on the road. When I arrived at the hospital, Ryan was rubbing his foot against the end of the bed. The gauze protecting one of his bedsores slipped off for the umpteenth time. The sitter summoned the nurse to put on a new bandage.

"You're making these nurses work, Ry," I joked, setting down my bag filled with thank-you notes I had to write and bills I had to pay.

Ryan's face twisted as if in pain.

"It was an accident," he said.

His words were soft and slurry but more understandable than just the day before.

"It's okay, Ryan," I said, stroking his arm. "I know it was an accident."

In the hallway, the nurse told me that when Ryan pulled the feeding tube out of his nose at 6:15 that morning, he was almost inconsolable. Later that morning, he was afraid to blow his nose for fear the tube might come out again.

"I don't want to take any chances," he told me.

He seemed to be dissolving in tears and apologizing all day, mostly about peeling the bandage off the scab on his head.

"I'm sorry!" Ryan kept saying as the square of gauze went flying across the room. "I don't want to."

When Lorna called after one of the scab episodes, he reached for the phone.

"Hi, Lorna," he said.

"How are you?" she asked.

"I feel bad," Ryan said and cried again about the bandage.

I told him that when he fell on his head, his brain got a little broken, just like a broken arm or a broken leg. I said that while it was healing, it was sending signals to his hand and arm to do things he really didn't want them to do. I assured him that everyone knew he didn't want to peel off the bandage. Everyone knew it was because of his fall.

I was wearing a baseball cap, and Ryan agreed it might be a good idea for him to wear it so that he couldn't get to the bandage so easily. He was wearing a T-shirt and basketball shorts from home. With the baseball cap, he looked like he was ready to leap out of bed and go to Eddie's Corner Grocery for a turkey-and-mayo sandwich and a root beer.

In less than five minutes, though, he tossed the cap on the floor and his hand went for the bandage. The sitter, a nice man named Henry, caught his arm before Ryan could reach his scalp.

"Thank you," Ryan said.

The hat toss became our scab alert. Ryan seemed relieved that we had figured out a way to help save him from himself.

Obviously the head injury was affecting his emotions. He took everything to heart. When he grabbed or pushed the sitter or the nurse in anger—usually as they were putting on the boots he hated or pulling a taped bandage from his skin—he apologized as soon as the pain or discomfort was over. He patted Kathy, his morning nurse, on her arm and stroked her face after getting mad at her for something or other.

"Thank you," he told her.

To help him sleep that afternoon, I read a story to him from *National Geographic Adventure* magazine. It was about three men who retraced the steps of the rugby players who had hiked out of the Andes after a plane crash. Ryan and I had watched the movie of the accident a while back. He fell asleep for a while, and when he woke up, I asked if he wanted me to pick up the story where we had left off.

"It's a sad story," he said. We decided not to read any more of it.

My mother called late in the afternoon. I put Ryan on the phone.

"Hi, Grandma," he said, clear as day.

Then: "Fine."

And: "I love you, too."

When I got the phone back, my mother was crying.

"I can't believe this," she said.

"I know." My throat hurt from trying not to cry.

The lucky Fatima rosary beads, the prayers, the crystal inside the deformed paper-clip holder Ryan made in kindergarten, the candles lighted in churches we had never seen, the energy from people we had never met, the love from our family and friends—do they have the power we always want to believe they have? I looked at how far Ryan had come in a month and couldn't help but think his battered head was not fighting this battle alone.

The next day, Ryan was approved to have ice chips. The speech therapist was close to approving him for water, but she didn't feel quite comfortable yet. You would have thought we were feeding Ryan milk shakes. He loved those ice chips.

The diarrhea had gotten worse. His sitter Regino didn't do any sitting: he was changing linens like a pit crew at the Daytona 500. Not surprisingly, Ryan had a rash to end all rashes. Every time he was cleaned up, he was in agony—only to have to go through the whole ordeal again twenty minutes later.

Barry and I waited until Ryan fell asleep around noon and walked to Haight Street for lunch and to find him a skullcap to replace the baseball cap. We wanted something soft that wouldn't be too hot and was comfortable enough to sleep in. Ryan seemed to like it, though he still pulled it off and tossed it across the room at regular intervals. He managed to peel the bandage off his scab just once. He seemed to be finding a bit more self-control.

He also showed us that he could raise his left arm to about ear level, though his hand didn't move at all yet. Hand movement required a lot more coordination and effort from the brain than the leg or the arm. The hand would be the last to "wake up," as I put it to Ryan.

We were exhausted when we left but drove to the Lindners' for dinner. We still couldn't face our empty house. And the Lindners, I knew, were grappling with their own fear and grief.

When we arrived at their house, their son, Scott, was holed up in his room downstairs. He didn't want to come up for dinner. He had reached a plea agreement that would send him to state prison for two years and three months in the incident that killed another boy. Scott was not required to report to prison until the judge handed down the official sentence, which was not expected for several months. But he had decided to turn himself in to county jail early because the months served there would reduce the time spent in the more horrifying environment of state prison.

I went downstairs and tapped on his door.

"It's Joan," I said.

In a thin voice, he told me to come in. The room was unlit, though not completely dark. Scott was in bed, under the covers. His face was drawn and pale; his eyes were red. He sat up and I hugged him. At eighteen, he still looked like the little boy who taught Ryan to write cursive at our kitchen table.

He asked about Ryan. I said he was doing better.

"I told your parents if there's anything we can do for you . . ." I said, fumbling to find something meaningful to say.

"You need to put all your energy into Ryan," Scott said. "Don't even think about me."

"Scott, I'm so sorry. I can't believe this is happening."

I hugged him again, we said good-bye, and I left before I began to cry. Halfway up the stairs to the kitchen, I broke down. Scott already seemed gripped by loneliness. He would have to walk down the cell block all by himself. His parents had to accept the awful truth that for the first time in their son's life, there was nothing they could do for him. They couldn't tape on a bandage or tuck him into bed with a cold compress.

I'm sure I was crying for Ryan as much as for Scott. What would happen to Ryan out in the world when we had to let go? Would he make good choices? Chris had done everything right, and still Scott made this devastating mistake. Would Ryan, like Scott, someday find himself facing the most terrifying moment of his life utterly alone? I was still haunted by my brother Bobby's loneliness, and my greatest worry every night was not about Ryan's health but that he would wake up in his hospital bed and look for us, and we wouldn't be there.

At dawn the next morning, as if Ryan had heard me, my cell phone rang as I was walking the dog. It was a nurse from UCSF.

"Your son wants to talk to you," she said. She handed the phone to Ryan.

"Mom," he said.

"Ry, is everything okay?"

"Mom," he said. "Come now. Come now."

He had woken up and we weren't there. He was cognizant enough now to notice our absence. He wanted us with him.

On our way into the city, Shirley from Kentfield Rehab called. She said everything was set for Ryan to move there that afternoon. We thought he wasn't moving until the following day. We were thrilled. We had two concerns, though.

Barry and I wondered if Ryan would feel frightened or depressed about going to Kentfield because it was the place where his grandmother, Barry's mother, had died. And we still worried that Ryan would be upset that he was so close to home but couldn't go there yet.

I rode with Ryan in the back of the ambulance from UCSF to Kentfield. He kept trying to yank off his helmet and pull the feeding tube out of his nose. I tried to distract him by narrating a travelogue: we were driving through Golden Gate Park, crossing the Golden Gate Bridge, passing through Sausalito, Mill Valley, Tiburon, Greenbrae, Kentfield.

"Home," Ryan said.

"Almost," I said. "We have to go to another hospital first to get you better."

Ryan had always been a homebody, a nester. He had made us promise never to sell our house because he was going to raise his own children in it. He insists on following family traditions, even if the traditions are news to Barry and me. Like poppy seed muffins on Christmas morning. We apparently had poppy seed muffins one Christmas morning and suddenly Ryan declared them a family tradition. We couldn't throw away any of his childhood toys or stuffed animals; he put them in plastic garbage bags and stored them in the rafters of the garage, waiting for his own children to play with them. On Friday nights when Barry was out of town, there was movie night: Ryan and I sprawled on the living room couch under chenille throw blankets eating pizza and popcorn off folding TV tables. He wouldn't think of doing anything else.

"Home," he said again.

"Almost."

It was September 18, a month and two days since the accident. We were, literally, steps from home. We had reached the last leg of this journey. Like Scott, we were marking time until our sentence was up.

Part III

Twenty-three

When the ambulance pulled into the lot of Kentfield Rehab, I saw the oak tree through the back window. I had forgotten how enormous and sprawling it was, how solid and stable. I couldn't help feeling hopeful at the familiar sight of it.

Ryan lay flat on the stretcher as the attendants unloaded him, his bony arms and legs tucked beneath a soft velour blanket we had brought from home. The black skullcap from Haight Street covered his misshapen head. His once-tanned, round face was now pale and gaunt. The thin feeding tube protruded from his nostril, forming a large loop between his nose and the spot on his cheek where the tube was taped; I had grabbed his wrist before he could pull it all the way out.

I followed the attendants as they wheeled Ryan down the long main hallway. We passed a woman slouched in a wheelchair, a wispy cloud of white hair sprouting from her pink scalp. She raised her head and smiled at us expectantly, as if she thought she might know us. Nurses in thick-soled shoes and loose, colorful tops padded in and out of rooms and hunched over medicine carts, counting pills into tiny paper cups. A youngish man, who turned out to be an ER doc paralyzed from the waist down in a biking accident, sat in his electric wheelchair at the end of the hall, tipped back as if doing a wheelie, typing on a laptop computer.

My eyes settled on the girl walking toward us. She looked to be a teenager. She clutched a teddy bear in one hand and her mother's arm in the other. She wore a foam rubber helmet like Ryan's. The left side of her face was crushed in, or maybe melted. There was a dark slit where her right eye should have been. Under the front of her helmet was an empty space on the left side. My breath caught. Half her skull and brain were gone, as if someone had scooped it out, leaving just a hairless concave scalp. The mother smiled at me as we passed.

Ryan's room had two empty beds. The ambulance attendants lifted him into the one closest to the sliding glass doors, which opened to a small courtyard of benches and flowerpots and a table with an umbrella. I pictured Ryan having lunch out there once he could sit in a wheelchair and eat real food.

"Ryan!"

I caught his arm as he reached again for the feeding tube.

"No! You don't want to do that."

The large loop, floating in front of his right eye, was impossible for him to ignore. No sooner had I pulled his hand away than it was up again, trying to yank it all the way out. I had expected a nurse or doctor to walk through the door at any moment to help me out. I waited, holding Ryan's straining arm as best I could as the ambulance attendants hung Ryan's IV bags, packed up their equipment, and handed me paperwork to sign.

Still no one showed up.

"We've got to get someone in here," I said, annoyed.

The attendants fetched a nurse and left.

"Okay," the nurse said, examining the feeding tube. "Hold his arms."

The nurse, a man in his forties, hunched over Ryan and slowly pushed the tube back into Ryan's nostril and down his throat.

"Swallow!" he told Ryan. "You need to swallow!"

Ryan thrashed like a mad man and opened his mouth in a silent scream.

"Ryan, Ryan. I'm sorry, sweetie. If you just let him do this, I'll give you all the ice chips you want," I said, my voice cracking. "Just swallow, baby."

Then inside Ryan's gaping mouth I saw why he was screaming.

"Stop! Stop! The tube is coiled in the back of his throat!"

The nurse, unperturbed, pulled the tube back out, hand over hand, as if he were raising a pail from a well. Ryan kicked and flailed. The nurse pressed the bedside button to summon help. Nothing. He pressed it again. A young woman, an aide, poked her head through the door.

"Need something?"

"Yes!" I said before the nurse could answer.

The aide grabbed hold of Ryan's left arm while I held the right. The nurse threaded the tube back through Ryan's nose.

"Swallow!" he said. "You have to swallow."

Ryan thrashed harder, his face twisted in pain. I wiped my tears on my shoulder, trying to control my voice and my breath, hating this ham-handed man hurting my son. Just get the fucking tube in.

"Almost done, sweetie," I choked out. "Swallow, baby. Swallow and you can have ice chips."

Another nurse arrived, a dread-locked middle-aged woman with a tie-dyed scarf swirled around her head.

"Mom, why don't you go wait outside," she said gently, lifting my hand from Ryan's arm. "We can do this."

In the hallway, I lit into the first person who looked like an administrator.

"How can I leave my son here when you can't even get a friggin' feeding tube in?"

I could barely get the words out. Barry had arrived from UCSF just as I was going off on the administrator. "What's going on?" he asked. Nurses and visitors had begun to linger in the hallway, watching the hysterical mother go ballistic. Later, after witnessing other parents break down in other hallways at Kentfield, I came to believe it was more compassion than curiosity that made people stop and watch. They recognized the sound and the look, the primitive barks and spews, the pained, unmasked face. You don't spend any time at a place like Kentfield Rehab and not know about breaking points.

Barry wrapped his arms around me, but I wriggled away and stalked down the hall into the parking lot. I hated that I had lost control and become the crazy, drama-queen, emotional wreck of a mother. I hated that my son had been put through such misery. I hated that the relief and well-being I felt in moving Ryan closer to home had been shattered.

I leaned against a fence on the bike path under the gnarled branches of the huge oak tree. A woman I know from Ross stopped her bike. I wiped my tears with the ends of my fingers and tried to tell her. But even to me, as I choked out the words, the feeding tube sounded so minor compared to what we had been through.

"You know he's going to be fine," my friend said, hugging me. "You've got to keep it together."

"Oh, I know," I said, taking a deep breath. "Just today . . . It was too much."

When I returned to Ryan's room, the feeding tube was in. The sitter had not yet arrived for the 3:00 P.M. shift, so for thirty minutes Barry and I were on our own, with the nurse in the tie-dyed scarf popping in and out. I asked her where I could get ice chips.

"I'll have to ask about that," she said.

The next thing I knew, the nursing supervisor was summoning me into the hallway. She said Ryan couldn't get ice chips until Kentfield's own speech therapist tested his swallowing capabilities.

"He was approved for ice chips at UCSF," I said. "Do you not trust the speech therapists at UCSF?"

"It's not about that. We just need to have our own therapist make the approval."

"Okay," I said, trying to control my voice. "What time is she coming?" The supervisor flipped a page on her clipboard.

"Tomorrow around two."

"Tomorrow? We need someone today. Now. I promised him ice chips."

"I'm sorry. She's not here until tomorrow."

"Tomorrow afternoon might not seem like a long time to you, but for someone who is dying for water, it's forever. This makes no sense. I want to talk to someone else."

I stomped back into Ryan's room, breathing like a bull. He was asleep, exhausted from the feeding tube fiasco.

"I hate this place," I said to Barry, wiping away more tears. "I can't leave Ryan here."

Barry went off to see what was going on. The tie-dyed nurse pulled a chair next to mine by Ryan's bed. She told me that Ryan was safe. She said there were lots of patients with feeding tubes and IVs and even ventilators, and the nurses had lots of experience, and I shouldn't judge on this one incident. It was a great hospital, she said. They would take good care of my son.

I know, I said. I'd always heard that. I wanted to believe her.

Then into the room walked a big, soft Haitian woman with a couple of gold teeth, a turban, and a bit of a swagger. She introduced herself as Clemania. She was Ryan's 3:00 to 11:00 P.M. sitter. Upon hearing the rundown of Ryan's situation, including the importance of keeping him from picking the scab on his scalp, she pronounced the task impossible. She could not be changing his sheets or his clothes and watching his hands at the same time. He needed to be in either restraints or mitts.

"The sitters at UCSF managed just fine," I said, trying to keep myself from crying again. "If you don't think you can do the job, we'll get someone else."

She squinted her eyes at me.

"I am keeping your son safe," she said.

She left the room and returned with big cotton mitts.

"He hates those," I said.

"He must wear them," she said.

Before I could say anything else, the nurse led me into the hallway.

"Clemania is the best sitter you could have gotten," she said. "Let her do her job."

I huffed back into the room. Clemania was changing the soiled bed linens and cleaning Ryan.

"Oooooh, I will clear up that rash. Don't worry," she said. "I am the queen of the diaper rash."

Ryan had been staring at Clemania from the moment she had arrived. He rubbed his mitted hand against his head. But he didn't complain.

"Me and you going to be all right together," Clemania told him. Then to me: "You go eat."

Barry and I left for dinner and returned around nine. We found Clemania in a chair by Ryan's bed. The mitts were off. Ryan was holding Clemania's hand. When he saw us in the doorway, he opened his arms. We hugged him, told him we loved him, and said we'd be back first thing in the morning.

"Call us for any reason," we told Clemania. We wrote all our phone numbers on the white board below the wall clock.

"Get some sleep," she said. "Ryan and me be fine. Won't we, baby?"

Ryan stroked Clemania's arm as if it were a soft blanket. He lifted her hand to rub it against his face.

I still wasn't sure about Clemania, but Ryan couldn't have been more content.

It was a different story when we arrived the next morning. He was so agitated he was sputtering.

"Ry, slow down," Barry said. "Say each word one at a time."

"He's . . . fucking . . . insane," Ryan said, pointing at his sitter, a young man working the morning shift. I stifled a laugh.

Ryan apparently didn't like the padding on the inside of his bed rails and was pulling them off. The sitter kept reattaching them, following doctor's orders. Even incidental bumps could damage a brain unprotected by skull bones.

Ryan's anger disappeared as quickly as it had erupted. We noticed he was more alert than he had been in days. His eyes opened wider; his words sounded clearer. His reflexes were quicker. He caught a small stuffed dog that I repeatedly and purposely threw off target. He had gotten five or six hours of sleep, the longest in two weeks. He was like a new guy.

His rehab officially began with a physical therapy session at eight that morning. With Barry on one side and the therapist, Hans, on the other, Ryan rose from the edge of the bed to his full height. He seemed to have grown during his month in bed. He looked queasy and unsteady as he held onto Barry and Hans and took a few steps to a chair and sat down. He said he had to go to the bathroom. He had been using a plastic urinal for peeing and a bedpan for bowel movements (when we could get it under him in time). Hans and Barry helped Ryan walk the five or six steps to the bathroom. For the first time since the accident, Ryan used the toilet.

The effort, though, made Ryan's head swim and his left knee hurt. (We didn't know if it had been injured in his skateboard accident or in a snowboard fall last winter.) His legs were like sticks, unable to bear the weight of his body. He had no muscle tone. Clearly, it would take a lot of work—and bulking up—to gain the strength to walk and run again. But even in that first session, he seemed so game. He never asked to go back to bed, despite his discomfort.

At two in the afternoon, as promised, the speech therapist arrived. She tested Ryan's swallowing and concluded he wasn't ready for water, but she relented on the ice chips.

A small triumph. Ice chips! We got ice chips!

As Ryan settled in for a nap, I asked him if he wanted me to sing to him. I did it often in ICU, singing the same songs I sang to him as a small child to help him sleep.

"No, thanks," Ryan said.

"You don't like my singing anymore?"

"No, I do."

"Then why don't you want me to sing to you?"

"It's embarrassing."

I laughed. It meant he was cognizant enough to know it was not exactly cool for your mother to be singing you to sleep at the age of sixteen.

Late that afternoon, Ryan got a roommate, an eighteen-year-old named Owen from Eureka, a town about five hundred miles north of the hospital. He had been in a car accident about six weeks earlier, in early August. He looked as if he had broken every bone in his face, including all of his teeth. His right hand was curled around a brace. He loped like John Wayne. When attendants set up his bed, they topped it with a zippered tent that resembled a mosquito net. He was a wanderer, as many brain-injured patients are. The tent kept him from getting out of bed at night.

"Hey, dude," Owen said, shaking Ryan's hand, then tapping fists.

"Hey, dude," Ryan said.

Owen was a talker who hugged everyone, including Ryan's visitors. He told us that he played football in high school. He showed us the get-well poster behind his bed from his old teammates and cheerleaders. In the center was a large photo of a good-looking, strong young man in a football uniform who looked nothing like the one now in the bed next to Ryan.

Owen told us that he had gotten his driver's license just a few weeks before the accident. He had picked up a friend late at night and had drifted across the center line. He had been so mangled that he was not expected to survive.

After dinner, Barry and I stopped on our way home to see Ryan (one of the great advantages of living so close). Clemania was his sitter again. I nodded and she nodded. I took off Ryan's mitts so that I could pull his T-shirt off. Then I helped him into a hospital gown. Clemania snapped a fresh sheet from a stack on the dresser, and as she rolled Ryan to one side, I stretched the sheet to the corners, then I rolled Ryan toward me, and Clemania finished on the other side. Then she lifted Ryan's hands to pull the mitts back on. I didn't say anything.

She said she was going to take a quick break while I was still there. Barry was down the hall in the bathroom.

I turned off the lights and lightly rubbed the edges of Ryan's ear between my fingers, something he had loved as a small child. A shaft of light from the hallway fell across his bed. Owen's television hummed on the other side of Ryan's curtain. I wondered how much of the trauma was registering, how much he might be homesick, how scared he was about his inability to walk or about the Jell-O-y feel of his head.

"So, Ryan, how has all this been for you?" I whispered.

"It's bad," he said matter-of-factly, his eyes locked on mine. He tapped a mitted hand onto the knit skullcap covering his scab, his substitute for scratching.

"But," he said, "it's okay."

At home, when Barry and I got into bed, Bill the dog left our bedroom to carry out his nightly ritual. He walked down the hall and turned left into Ryan's room. He looked at the bed where he normally slept, sniffed around, walked out, and returned back down the hall. Then he jumped onto our bed and curled up, settling yet again for us.

I had my own ritual. Most mornings I went into Ryan's bedroom to check on his boa constrictor, his bearded dragon, and his leopard gecko. They lived in separate glass aquariums on Ryan's dresser and desk. Ozzie, the beardie, would lift his prehistoric head, on alert. The boa, six feet long and thick as a Sunday roast, would ignore me. The gecko hid under a shell. I'd pour water through the screens and into their water bowls. I'd make sure the lizards still had crickets. I'd remind myself to defrost one of the rats we kept in the freezer for the snake. Then I'd smooth out the already smooth white down comforter on Ryan's bed.

On his second full day at Kentfield, Ryan was cleared to eat puréed food. He still could not drink water. His brain still wasn't responding quickly enough to keep the water from sliding down his trachea instead of the esophagus.

Ryan was not as excited as I thought he would be about the food. He ate ice cream and pudding with some interest but wasn't crazy about the thickened fruit juice and puréed meals. I asked Clemania what the brownish muffin on Ryan's plate was. She picked it up, tore off a piece, and brought it to her nose.

"Meat." She rolled her eyes.

Rana from Café Marmalade in Ross sent over puréed pears and puréed veggies. Ryan liked them, but he became full so fast.

The bad news was that a barium and X-ray test showed that enough water from the ice chips was still trickling into his lungs to put him at risk for pneumonia. So no more ice chips.

Ryan was, predictably, obsessed with water. He said he dreamed about it. When, by the third day at Kentfield, he was strong enough to take jaunts around the hospital, propelling the wheelchair by pushing his feet against the floor, he took sharp lefts and rights toward every sink and water fountain.

"Just a sip," he'd say as we steered him away. In the cafeteria, he chugged over to the soda machine, opened his arms, and hugged it.

When we took him outside to see Bill for the first time one morning, he gave his dog a cursory scratch behind the ear, then pointed to a hose behind a bench.

*Outside Kentfield
Rehab, Ryan, in
a wheelchair with
a feeding tube
and a protective
helmet, greets his
dog, Bill, for the
first time in five
weeks.*

"Bill wants that water," he said.

Because we had to be ruthless about the water, we let Ryan get away with other things. I'd slip him ice chips now and again. And we didn't make him wear the mitts, which he had come to hate. We kept a close eye on his hands and required him to wear his knit cap, so he rarely reached the scab. Even Clemania gave in on the mitts. She had become as much of a pushover with him as we had.

She cleared up the diaper rash, true to her word, but now Ryan had a new source of misery—besides the scab on his scalp and the bedsores on his heels. It began when I was massaging balm into his dry feet.

"Mom! My toes! Don't touch my toes!" he cried, throwing his head back and writhing in pain.

He said the toes on his left foot felt as if bricks were crushing them. We were told it might be nerve damage or maybe the brain sending errant pain signals. But all that day and for weeks to come, Ryan warned everyone who entered his room, "Don't touch my toes!" The person might be there to empty the trash bins. "Don't touch my toes!" Ryan would cry. Changing the bandages on his bedsores became a protracted exercise in cajoling and soothing, starting and stopping. Pulling his pants on and off had to be approached with the delicacy of a surgeon.

I gave him a dry-erase board and a marker so that he could make a sign to hang over his bed.

"Attention," he wrote. "Don't touch my toes."

The words trailed down the board in shaky letters of diminishing size and legibility, like a castaway's note in the sand.

Twenty-four

B arry's cell phone rang at 7:30 one morning, less than a week after Ryan arrived at Kentfield.

"Dad, where are you? Come over."

Barry rushed out. Ryan was in bed. He didn't need anything. He just wanted to see his dad. He was chatty and sharp, the result, we presumed, of having a decent night's sleep.

Despite that awful first day at Kentfield, Ryan was making remarkable progress. He was getting in and out of the wheelchair on his own. He could straighten the fingers on his left hand and lightly grasp a cup of applesauce while he spooned it out with his right hand. He was approved to eat "mechanically chopped food" instead of puréed foods: muffin and omelet for breakfast, chicken salad sandwich for lunch, and chopped chicken, baked yams, and chocolate cake for dinner! What a wonderful thing. His favorite, though, was the butterscotch pudding Lorna brought every single afternoon, one for Ryan and one for Owen.

Every morning, Ryan worked with an occupational therapist who helped him relearn how to dress, brush his teeth, use the bathroom on his own, perform the daily tasks of living. In physical therapy, he already was taking steps with a walker. One day late in that first week, I watched him walk, clutching the walker, with a labored gait and intense concentration, two hundred feet toward an exit sign at the end of a hallway. With about fifty feet to go, clearly exhausted, he drifted off course, inching toward the side wall. Hans, his therapist, gently reminded him to point himself toward the exit sign. Ryan looked up and righted himself, reaching the finish line just before collapsing back into his wheelchair.

Ryan was quickly becoming a star at the hospital, a favorite of the nurses, sitters, and therapists for his politeness and willingness to work hard. Barry and I weren't faring as well.

The hospital's director of the traumatic brain injury program called us into her pin-neat office one day. She was a slender, attractive woman with long dark hair and a slight stoop in her bearing, giving her a look of someone at the starting line of a road race. She was one of the best at what she did. So when you had a meeting with her, you sat and listened and nodded a lot, completely thankful she was in charge of your kid's future.

She told us in no uncertain terms that Ryan was to wear the mittens at *all* times so that he couldn't pick the scab on his head. Did we *understand* the serious risk? Did we *want* his brain to get infected? And he could not under *any* circumstances have ice chips. Her priority, she said, was to keep him safe, and she would *think* that would be our priority, too. Rehab was meaningless, wasn't it, if Ryan landed back in the hospital with pneumonia.

And another thing, she said. Cut down on Ryan's visitors. He had limited physical and cognitive energy. He should be spending it on rehab. One hour a day for visitors, preferably between 6:30 and 7:30 P.M. Had she made herself clear?

Barry and I nodded like bobble-heads.

I asked Ryan every day how he was doing. Mostly he would say fine. One day he said, "Good, but not as good as a week ago."

I asked why.

"I feel immobile and I don't have my dog."

As Ryan's brain rebooted, he began to make strange comments.

"Mom, I think I was just on TV," he said when I walked into his room one day. "In a race."

Just then my cell phone rang. It was Doug, Lorna's husband, wishing me a happy birthday from London. Ryan asked for the phone.

"Am I on television there?" Ryan asked him.

Later I mentioned to Ryan that he had been asleep for two weeks after his accident. He looked startled.

"Boy, I've slept a long time before, but never two *weeks*," he said.

"And hopefully you won't sleep for two weeks again," I said.

"You never know."

He once noticed me writing notes. On the loudspeaker came the announcement, "Dr. Westin, Dr. Westin."

"Write that down," Ryan said helpfully. "Dr. Westin, Dr. Westin."

One afternoon, he thought I had pulled a bandage off his leg. I said there had been no bandage. He insisted. He said it hurt and that his hair had come off. I had found it made more sense to go along with his fantasies than try to convince him what was real.

"I'll put some balm on it, okay?"

"But," he said, still alarmed, "who's going to put the hair back?"

His brain seemed like a bin of random items, a repository of images real and imagined, past and present, and he had no mechanism for sorting and categorizing, or for storing any of them in his memory. Once, when he asked to use the toilet, I explained that he was hooked up to an IV at the moment. There was no nurse around to disconnect it. He would have to use the plastic urinal. He asked again, and I explained again about the IV. I handed him the urinal, and he handed it back.

"Ryan, do you understand why you can't use the bathroom?"

"Because it's not my bathroom?"

He had no recollection, for example, of his calls to us at dawn, which had become daily occurrences. By afternoon, if the phone call was mentioned, he vehemently denied ever making it.

Before the end of his first week, the feeding tube was pulled from Ryan's nose and the PICC line from his arm. He was finally unfettered. When his PICC line came out (a weird thing to watch, like pulling a tapeworm from somebody's arm) Ryan bled, dripping huge blots onto his shorts and the linoleum floor. The nurse's aide quickly covered the bleed with gauze, and it stopped almost immediately.

"I'm still bleeding," Ryan said, though there was no more blood.

"Why do you say that?" I asked.

"By the fact that I'm bleeding."

I wondered what it was like inside his head, if it felt as if he were in an unfamiliar world that required him to figure out, from the clues around him, where he was and how this world operated. I heard him one day describing the hospital to his friend Nate. Ryan was on a cell phone and propelling himself in his wheelchair through the halls. He passed the rehab gym, where he noticed a stationary bicycle.

"Our beds have bicycles in them," I heard Ryan tell Nate. "You can ride your bed down the hall."

I occasionally asked Ryan what he remembered about the accident. I knew the brain injury wiped out all memory of that afternoon and his weeks at UCSF. But I wanted to see what scenario he had constructed for himself.

"I'm pissed off at that hill," he told me one day. "I want to go down it again. It's not that dangerous a hill. I think it was me. It was my fault. I didn't turn enough.

"Everything was fine until I got past the Ballards' house. I started to tail-bend. The back of the skateboard started to shake. I would have made it, too, if I had gotten past the fence. If I had gotten past the construction site. I would have made it fine."

The street he was describing was Bridge, not Lagunitas, where the accident actually occurred.

I told him that some neighborhood boys witnessed the accident and that one, John Hansen, had called 911. John's quick thinking might have saved his life, I said.

"Well," Ryan said. "I will have to thank John Hansen."

I asked what he remembered of the ambulance.

"I remember the guys being really nice. I remember the driver was insane. The ambulance dude drove like there was no tomorrow. He was just crazy."

I stayed around one day when Linda, Ryan's speech therapist, tried to assess his thinking skills.

"If you found the door open and the lock broken at your home, what would you do?" Linda asked.

"I'd get a knife from the kitchen and go upstairs," Ryan said. He explained that he would want to stop the robber.

"What if the robber had a gun? Would going upstairs with a knife be a very safe thing to do?"

"I could get a gun, too," Ryan said.

After some prompting, Ryan decided calling "the cops" on his cell phone was the most logical and prudent course.

"I'm doing this because I need to see if your brain is working with good judgment," Linda said.

"My brain never worked with good judgment," Ryan replied, smiling.

Linda then quizzed him on word meanings to see how facile his mind was. She asked what *ring* meant. Ryan said a telephone ring.

"What else?" Linda asked.

"A ring around a finger. A ring around a toilet or bathtub."

"What if you added *ing*? Ringing?"

"Wringing somebody's neck," Ryan said. "Ringing a horseshoe."

I'm not sure about Linda, but I was impressed.

"What about the word *plant*?"

Ryan came up with plant your feet down, plant flowers. Linda asked what the word might mean if he were a spy. Ryan said planting a spying device. Then he came up with a nuclear plant.

Next Linda gave him four words and asked him to identify the one that didn't belong. Shirt, pants, leg, hat.

"Shirt," Ryan said. Linda explained why the right answer was leg.

"Susan, Mary, John, Karen."

"John."

"Giraffe, pencil, orangutan, tiger."

"Orangutan."

"Why an orangutan?" Linda asked.

Because it was a mammal, Ryan said. But he understood when Linda went over the words again and guided him through the logic.

"Root beer, hamburger, french fries, salad."

"Salad."

It wasn't the right answer for Linda, but for Ryan it made sense. The first three went together in a meal that Ryan would actually eat. The salad didn't.

In occupational therapy later in the day, Ryan used his weak left hand to place wooden pegs of varying sizes into an upright board filled with holes of varying sizes. The slender pegs kept slipping out of his fingers. He had a hard time inserting them in the right-size holes.

"Can I go back to my room now?" Ryan asked. He had been awake the night before from 11:00 to 6:30. He was beat.

"We have five more minutes," the therapist said. "Can we do one more exercise?"

"Okay."

By the end of that first week at Kentfield, I was so tired I had stopped taking notes and was posting only the most cursory entries on the blog we had begun about two weeks after the accident. I had been posting summaries of each day, usually as I sat in bed around 11:00 P.M. I loved reading the encouraging comments from friends and relatives as far away as Dubai and Tanzania, Washington, D.C., and New York. Some left comments every day, letting us know we were always in their thoughts.

I think because Ryan was doing so well, I finally could relax, and suddenly the fatigue set in. I thought every afternoon about escaping home for a nap. But the truth was I loved spending time with Ryan. It was like watching your baby progress through the stages of development on time-lapse film. It was riveting.

And aside from his physical pain, Ryan was a complete joy, all please and thank-you and hugs and kisses. Maybe a brain injury accentuated certain parts of a person's personality, and this injury happened to accentuate Ryan's kind spirit.

The nurses and sitters stopped in even when they weren't assigned to him to say hi, get a hug, and see how he was doing. He somehow remembered all their names. He especially loved Clemania.

"How's my baby?" she'd say when she arrived for her shift. Her skin was as soft and smooth as rose petals, and Ryan—always a texture guy—could spend an hour just stroking her face and arms. I had come to love Clemania, too, recognizing what I had not that first day at Kentfield when I thought she was imperious and inflexible for insisting on Ryan wearing mitts. She protected her patients, even if that meant staring down a mother like me. Clemania took care of Ryan as if he were her own child.

We knew Ryan's sweetness was likely to turn. He probably would become agitated and even explosive as physical therapy became more rigorous and he became more aware of how his life had changed. That is generally what happens in the recovery process for brain-injured people, and we were seeing it with his roommate, Owen. He had become so abusive to the staff that

the hospital's psychologist imposed a behavior plan that involved gold stars on a chart. He lost certain privileges—such as
the wristband that allowed him to roam the halls on his own—
for swearing and belligerence. He saved his worst behavior for
his mother.

Wendy was a vivacious manicurist who was sleeping at a local
trailer park in a camper borrowed from her ex-husband's parents.
It allowed her to be close to the hospital without having to spend
money on a hotel. When the ex-husband drove down to Marin
for the weekend, they had to share the camper. But Wendy always
put up a good front, even in the midst of Owen's tirades.

"Get out!" Owen would shout at her out of nowhere. "You're
a fucking idiot! Go away!"

He criticized the food she brought, the T-shirts she bought
for him, the speed at which she summoned the nurse for his pain
meds. Wendy mostly shrugged and smiled. But sometimes when
we went for walks on the bike trail, she broke down.

"I can't do this," she'd say. "I know it's the brain injury, but
he's so horrible to me. What's the point of being here for him?"

Her ex-husband told the hospital he wanted to take Owen
home instead of continuing with rehab. The hospital was recom-
mending that Owen move to a facility in Southern California that
teaches brain-injured adults how to live independently. Wendy
knew Owen wasn't capable of getting a job and taking care of
himself. He was a long way from it. And if he didn't get the help
now, he might never get any better. Owen, of course, agreed with
his dad. He wanted out. He wanted to have a beer when he felt
like it and go outside without having to show he had the right
wristband.

I looked at Owen and wondered when Ryan's anger might kick
in. Ryan had something of a trash mouth most of his life, despite
my attempts to break the habit by dabbing Tabasco on his tongue
as a kid. But so far in this ordeal, Ryan had been the sweetest kid
in the world. We were enjoying every moment.

"You're amazing, Ryan," I said one morning.

"No, you're amazing," he said, and kissed me on the cheek.

"Before the accident, you didn't kiss," I said. "You've always been a great hugger, but you never kissed, except when you were really, really sorry."

"Well," Ryan said, smiling. "I'm really, really sorry."

Twenty-five

Every corridor at Kentfield Rehab was a roll call of devastation. I understood now what I had been told at Walter Reed Military Hospital, where I researched my series about wounded soldiers: no matter how bad you have it, someone else has it worse.

Niki, the young woman in the helmet who I had seen walking with her mother, was in a room down the hall from Ryan and Owen. She had been one class away from graduating from California State University at Chico. In photos on the wall by her bed, she was a pretty, dark-haired young woman with her arms looped around the shoulders of girlfriends. One afternoon in June, she went out on a boat with friends from college. Most were drinking. Niki wasn't a drinker, and witnesses later said she hadn't been drinking at all that day. One of the friends was wakeboarding behind the boat. When he fell off the board, the boat's driver made a U-turn to retrieve him. But the turn was so sharp that half the passengers were thrown overboard. Niki was one of them.

The boat's propeller caught Niki's head, lopping off her left eye and much of the left side of her brain. She was given almost no chance of survival. Her parents prayed. Their church held vigils. She pulled through and now was at Kentfield. She couldn't speak except for some low guttural sounds. She didn't understand much of what was said. She couldn't smile. But she could walk. So almost any time of day and early evening, we saw Niki and her mother, Cindy, walking the halls or the bike trail.

Cindy was outgoing and cheerful, almost bubbly. Her only child was alive. She could hug her and kiss her and stroke her hair. Cindy was sure that, in time, the undamaged right side of her daughter's brain would compensate for what was missing from the left side. She had heard that can happen. So, she believed, even though Niki's speech center was gone, she would speak again. Cindy was at Niki's side all day, every day, chatting away, telling her about the dogs they passed on the bike trail, pointing out the trees that were beginning to turn red and gold. She never showed signs of fatigue, though she drove an hour each way from her brother's house in Napa. Her husband visited on the weekends from their home three hours away in Chico.

At places like Kentfield, all the parents eventually meet. We strike up conversations in the hallways and lobby, commiserating without prying, talking in medical acronyms and referencing pharmaceuticals and dosages as if we had become adjunct staff. Darlene had it tougher than any of us, even tougher than Cindy. Her only child, Josh—what was it with only children and devastating accidents?—had been a passenger in a car that crashed. He was twenty. You could still see the square jaw and broad shoulders of the athletic young man he once had been. His brain injury left him in a semivegetative state. He was bedridden and on a ventilator and a feeding tube. He couldn't speak. He could barely move. His pale, empty eyes stared straight ahead, except when they drifted in slow motion toward some mysterious point in the middle distance.

Darlene was a thirty-something single mother with Peggy Lipton–blond hair and sharp cheekbones. She was bone thin, as if grief had gnawed away at everything inside her. She smoked in the parking lot with the nurses' aides. She slept in Josh's room most nights. She and Josh had been at Kentfield longer than any of us. She cried more easily than we did, surely from exhaustion. But she also bounded around the hospital sometimes, visiting Owen, Ryan, and Niki, kissing their cheeks and pulling them to her in tight hugs. When she asked how Ryan was doing, I found myself downplaying his progress. I couldn't imagine what it was like for her to see everyone else moving forward, however incrementally, and Josh lying there blank-eyed, day after day.

Around the corner from Josh was a man who never stopped moaning.

"Ma-*maaa*! Ma-*maaa*!"

Ryan said he sounded like a Wookie from *Star Wars*.

"Ma-*maaa*! Ma-*maaa*! Ma-*maaa*! Ma-*maaa*!"

The man's door was always open, but the curtain around his bed was pulled, so we never saw him when we passed by. Clemania told me that he was in his thirties and had suffered a severe brain injury in a motorcycle accident. He had a wife and a young child who lived several hours away. His wife's visits had dwindled steadily in the months he had been at Kentfield. No one had seen her in a while. The man's relentless moaning prevented him from having a roommate, so he spent every day in his room alone, calling for his mother.

I ventured into the Wookie's room one day when his curtain was open, in part from curiosity, in part to see if he just wanted some company. He was sitting in his wheelchair, his hands tied to the chair's arms. His head lolled to the side.

"Ma-*maaa*!" he said, eyeing me. Then: "Take these off!" He strained against the straps on his wrists.

I asked his name and if there was something I could do other than untie him. "I have a little boy," he said. "He plays soccer. He was here yesterday. Come sit on my lap." He licked his lips.

I said I'd check in on him again. "Wait! Wait! Just untie these. Just for a minute. Just for a minute."

When I left, he fell quiet. Maybe he was waiting for me to come back. Then: "Ma-*maaa!* Ma-*maaa!*"

I told Clemania that night about my visit with the Wookie.

"Life doesn't get much worse than that," I said.

She told me to follow her. She took me to the room next to the Wookie. She flipped on the light and there in the bed was an older version of Niki. The left side of the man's brain was missing, as if it had been scooped out with a big spoon and his scalp had been laid back inside the crater. His eyes were half open. Clemania said he couldn't speak and didn't seem to recognize anyone. She thought he had had a brain tumor, but she wasn't sure.

She pulled the door shut and we headed back to Ryan's room.

"You are lucky, lucky, lucky," she said. "I hope you thank God every day."

Dr. Deborah Doherty, the chief of the brain trauma unit, stopped in often to check on Ryan. At the end of the first week, she was asking Ryan to tell her the year and the month, how many fingers she was holding up, what came next in the sequence, 1-A-2-B. Ryan nailed almost all of her questions (though the sequence question thoroughly confounded him). His speech was clearer than she had heard it before. His mobility was greater. His energy level was higher. He didn't seem at all like someone who had been bedridden just a week earlier.

She took us into the hallway.

"He's doing really great," she said, shaking her head. "Really great."

But he still wasn't close to drinking water. He gagged almost every time he took a sip with the speech therapist; the water still was going down the wrong pipe.

The next morning, I watched Ryan in the occupational therapy room. He was asked to lift wooden puzzle pieces with his left hand—the one that wasn't moving a week ago—and fit them into the matching slots. Each piece had a small handle, similar to pre-school puzzles.

He stiffly grasped a yellow one in the shape of a square. With great effort and concentration, he lined the puzzle piece up with the square hole and guided it through. Later, to increase the range of motion in his left shoulder, he slid discs from one side of an arch to the other and then back again.

One of the therapists slipped out into the hall to stand next to me.

"What a difference four days makes," she said. "He couldn't do any of this last week. It's unbelievable. Helps to be sixteen."

With Hans, the physical therapist, Ryan walked on his own—slowly, deliberately—out of his room, down two hallways, out the back door, and across the outside deck. Hans kept his hand an inch from Ryan's back, ready to catch him if he stumbled.

"You can sit down for a minute, or you can keep going," Hans said.

"Keep going," Ryan said.

Yessss.

I wanted to burst sometimes when I watched him. Almost from the moment Ryan woke from his coma, Barry and I found ourselves standing in admiration, even awe, of our son. It was not, frankly, a familiar experience. We were the parents at birthday parties with paper towels and brooms, promising to replace the vase or to pay for the carpet cleaning. We were the parents who prayed for one base hit before the season's end, for one night of homework without a meltdown. In all the conventional ways society measures children, Ryan came up short. Now, here in this place, he was remarkable, a kid you'd invent if you could. He was unfailingly cheerful (except about his toes, and now his left foot was hurting, too). He seemed to accept everything demanded of him. He didn't complain. He was loving and good-humored and resilient. Maybe most of all, resilient. Maybe he was handling all this so well because he was accustomed to struggling. Few things in his life had come easily.

We returned home every night marveling at the spirit of our kid. One of our friends described Ryan as a "gentle warrior." That captured him perfectly.

Ryan was surpassing everybody's expectations, not just ours. People began saying he was a miracle boy. At Marin General, where Ryan was transported one afternoon for a routine CT scan, a nurse asked if my son was the one who had the skateboard accident. She said she had been in the ER the night he came in.

"I thought about you all the way home that night," she said. "I can't believe this is the same kid."

When Ryan emerged from the CT scan, two more nurses had joined the first one in the hallway. They had been either in the ER or in ICU with Ryan. They watched him roll by on the gurney. He was chatting and laughing with the EMT about cars. One nurse clapped her hand to her mouth.

"What an inspiration," she said.

Dr. Doherty at Kentfield was equally impressed. On Ryan's tenth day at the rehab hospital, we sat in her office as she summarized the dramatic progress he had made: the scab on his scalp was 90 percent healed; he was off the feeding tube and now was eating chopped food; he needed minimal assistance for personal hygiene, sitting up and standing. She was still concerned about his impulsivity: getting out of bed without anyone there to help him, for instance, and pulling the bandages off his bedsores.

"I'm afraid he's a danger to himself because he moves fast and does things that are not always in his best interest," she said. And while his memory for names and faces was "remarkable," his "procedural memory" was weak. He couldn't remember the steps he had been taught to carry out even simple tasks like getting dressed or transferring safely to his wheelchair.

Her team's consensus, Dr. Doherty said, was that he would be ready to go home in four to six weeks. She disagreed with the team. She thought it would be one-third to one-half that time.

"He's flying through rehab," she said.

Barry and I wheeled Ryan onto the wooden deck that overlooked the bike trail. Ryan's sitter brought his lunch tray; Barry and I brought sandwiches. It seemed a turning point. All the major medical issues, except replacing the bone flaps, were behind us. Ryan was "flying." I thought about Owen and how he might never be better than he was right then, how Josh was still in a vegetative state, how Niki couldn't speak or understand most of what was said. We were lucky, lucky, lucky.

Twenty-six

The first sign that something was wrong was the wooden pegs slipping from his fingers.

In occupational therapy one afternoon, Ryan had a hard time inserting the pegs in the right-size holes, a task he had mastered a week earlier.

"Can I go back to my room now?" he asked. He was beat.

"We have five more minutes," the therapist said. "Can we do one more exercise?"

"Okay."

We wrote off his struggles as an off day. But the next day he was worse. He started the morning by swearing at the nurse and aide for touching his foot. His pain seemed to have escalated not only in his toes but his knee. Even with a soft brace on his knee, he had trouble standing for physical therapy. His fairly confident walk of a few days ago now was halting and stumbling, like a drunk listing to the left.

Ryan looked weak and unsteady. He was lethargic. He was sleeping more. His speech had slowed, not dramatically but enough to notice. Maybe, we thought, it was the Tylenol with codeine he was taking for pain. We also noticed a slight bulge on the left side of his head where the skull was missing. It felt like a water balloon. Dr. Doherty said she'd keep an eye on it.

Barry and I were in the parking lot of Home Depot when the call came. We had been about to choose carpet for the garage, which we were turning into a hangout space for Ryan. It was Mark Eastham, the famous Dr. Doom from Marin General. Though he was no longer Ryan's neurosurgeon, he still followed Ryan's progress.

He said he had reviewed the CT scan Ryan had had at Marin General several days earlier. The scan alarmed him. There was swelling in the ventricles, including the third ventricle. It should look like a ribbon and instead looked like a lightbulb. And, he said, Ryan had a new hemorrhage on the right side.

We wondered why, if the results were so worrisome, Dr. Gupta from UCSF hadn't called us. We knew Gupta had the CT scan— we had hand-delivered it to his office ourselves. Eastham invited us down to Marin General to review the scan. He'd show us what he was talking about.

Bill Gonda, Ryan's pediatrician, was already at Marin General when we arrived. He had canceled an appointment to be there, and he looked as worried as Eastham. In a small office off the emergency room, we leaned over Eastham's shoulder to look once again at a picture of our son's brain. The ventricles were noticeably larger. The new hemorrhage, like the one that very first night in the ER, looked like nothing, a smudge, a drop of water on the film.

Dr. Eastham had a theory about what was happening. He said Ryan had become hydrocephalic, meaning his brain's mechanism for reabsorbing fluid never kicked in after the accident.

Hydrocephalus, also known as water on the brain, is actually a buildup of cerebrospinal fluid inside the brain. The body produces about a pint of the fluid every day. It circulates throughout the brain and down the spinal cord, protecting the nervous system. The fluid is then reabsorbed, and more fluid is produced. If the fluid builds up, it can damage the brain the way swelling can: the brain is squeezed because the skull allows no room for expansion. In Ryan's brain, the increased fluid was creating enough pressure to stretch the blood vessels, and one of the stretched vessels had ruptured, Eastman said.

Ryan's slight regression and fatigue, and the small bulge of fluid on his left side, were corroborating evidence that he had hydrocephalus, he said. The ventricles needed to be drained immediately to prevent further hemorrhaging. And Ryan probably needed a shunt.

We called Gupta, but by the time we went to bed that night, we still had not heard from him. We talked to Dr. Manley from San Francisco General, though, and he said that from what we had described, the hemorrhage wasn't likely to cause immediate harm, given that Ryan had only minor symptoms of hydrocephalus. And he assured us that if Dr. Gupta had seen anything he thought was worrisome, he would have called by now. I had a queasy feeling for the first time in weeks. I hoped Manley was right, that Gupta's reading of Ryan's CT scan was different from Eastham's and there was nothing to worry about.

When Gupta called the next morning, Tuesday, October 4, he said he understood Eastham's concerns but that it was premature to conclude Ryan was hydrocephalic. The ventricles were enlarged for several possible reasons, none of which required immediate action. In severe brain injuries like Ryan's, the damaged part of the brain dies and is absorbed into the body. Because nature abhors a vacuum, cranial spinal fluid fills the vacated space. Also, he explained, if the brain loses enough volume from the damage, the entire brain is smaller, and thus the ventricles appear to be larger. And, he said, the ventricles might be plumper with fluid simply because they can be: the skull isn't there as a bulwark to contain their expansion.

Gupta said he was reassured by what the CT scan showed about the surface of Ryan's brain. It still had crevices. A truly hydrocephalic brain would be so full it would have flattened out the crevices. And Dr. Doherty had reported to him that Ryan's brain was still soft, confirming that the pressure had not reached a dangerous level.

As for the hemorrhage, Gupta said it was about a half-inch in diameter and close to the surface. He figured Ryan got it from bumping his head rather than from the internal pressure stretching the blood vessels. He said he wanted to get Ryan's bone flaps back on as soon as possible, perhaps as early as the following week, to prevent more bumps and more hemorrhages. The scalp wound, of course, had to be completely healed, and it was 95 percent there.

I called Manley and asked him to look at Ryan's CT scan, too. He did and he agreed with Gupta. There was no need for a shunt just yet. So we decided to do nothing. We would wait and see.

Back at Kentfield Rehab, we posted signs around Ryan's bed to make sure he had cushioning on the bed rails at all times and for everyone to be especially vigilant about putting on Ryan's helmet whenever he was out of bed.

I wanted, of course, to believe that everything was more or less fine. But there was no denying that Ryan no longer was "flying" through rehab. For the rest of the day, he was either in pain or he was sleeping. In his wheelchair, his left foot trailed behind his right as he struggled to push himself down the hall. Just a week earlier, he was moving so fast in his chair we had to holler at him to slow down. After physical therapy at 3:30, he fell straight asleep and didn't wake up until early evening.

"Of course, it could be the codeine," I said to Barry when we slipped away for dinner.

"Or the Neurontin," he said. Dr. Doherty had increased Ryan's dosage to help with the neuropathic pain in his toes.

"Just the pain itself can be exhausting," I said.

Two days later, Ryan was back in ICU at UCSF.

Dr. Doherty had called an ambulance when she saw that Ryan had been too tired for any of his therapies and had barely eaten anything in twenty-four hours. By the time he arrived at UCSF, he was so lethargic we could barely rouse him. He no longer was moving his left hand. When he did talk, his words were slurred. He had a temperature of 100.3. He had diarrhea again.

A CT scan at UCSF showed that the ventricles had filled even more and that the fluid collecting on the left side between the scalp and the brain membrane had increased. Dr. Gupta viewed the scan from home and instructed the resident to drain the bulging pocket of fluid from the left side. Half a soda can's worth of fluid came out. But within hours, the site began to bulge again. The fluid had come right back.

It turned out Eastham was right. Ryan was hydrocephalic.

Dr. Gupta took him into surgery the next day and inserted a shunt. The shunt is a silicon tube as thin as a strand of spaghetti. One end of the tube is in Ryan's right brain ventricle. It then snakes up to the scalp, runs just under the skin down his neck and chest, and ends in his abdominal cavity, where the fluid is deposited. The flow of fluid is controlled by a valve the size of an almond that is tucked under Ryan's scalp. He will have it the rest of his life.

It's amazing what can become the focus of the day. Here was a kid with a severe brain injury, and the biggest concerns during the last month had been diarrhea, rashes, sore toes, a creaky knee, a scab, bedsores, IV placements, and feeding tubes.

The day after the shunt went in, the all-consuming issue was peeing.

Ryan couldn't.

He had been having trouble in this area for days. He would need twenty or thirty minutes before anything happened. A bedside scan showed his bladder was beyond full. So, finally, the nurses inserted a catheter, which Ryan hated, hated, hated. He peed out almost 1,000 cc, which is nearly a quart, or at least it looks that way in the plastic container.

"I feel like I peed out a baby," he said.

The nurses promised that if Ryan needed a catheter again that night, they would sedate him and give him lidocaine. At 9:00 P.M., the resident came in to see if Ryan had peed on his own. Ryan had been holding the plastic urinal in a receiving position for about twenty minutes, trying to will his body to cooperate.

"I'll give you another ten, then we'll have to discuss other options," she said.

Ryan knew what that meant.

"Fifteen minutes," he said.

She said okay.

I was convinced Ryan had a urinary tract infection and wasn't going to pee. So I reminded him about the sedation and the lidocaine.

"The catheter won't hurt, and I'll distract you while they're doing it," I said.

"Will you dance?"

I said I would.

As the words came out of my mouth, I heard the lovely, wondrous pitter-patter of urine hitting the inside of the plastic container. I saw the look of sheer pleasure and relief on Ryan's face. I took the container to the nurses' station, where the doctor and nurse were figuring out how best to deal with putting in the catheter.

"We have liftoff!" I said, holding up the urinal.

A small triumph.

The shunt clearly was working. The front of Ryan's head was now almost concave. I could see the edges of the skull where the bone had been cut away. He still had a pocket of fluid on the right side, though. That might need to be tapped to make it disappear.

Two days after the insertion of the shunt, Ryan was using his left hand again and no longer listing to the left. His eyes were bright. He was rocking out to the ring tone on Barry's cell phone, the "Alligator Boogaloo." Ryan made us call the cell phone repeatedly so he could do the sitting-in-bed version of *Dance Fever*.

Ryan was well enough to return to Kentfield Rehab that day, but much to our frustration, a communications glitch between the insurance company and the two hospitals kept him in ICU. When Barry's voice started to rise in talking to one of the administrators, Ryan said, "Dad, it's all right. It's all right."

While we were allowing ourselves to be irritated by the transfer snafu, an alarm sounded. A red light began to pulse on the wall above the nurses' station. The glass-enclosed rooms were arranged in a horseshoe, with the nurses' station in the center. I looked out Ryan's sliding glass door. Everyone on staff was rushing to a room at the far end of the horseshoe. I heard someone on the phone saying that a cardiac nurse was needed right away. Ryan's nurse quickly closed our door and pulled the curtain across the glass so we couldn't see. Still, I could hear someone on the phone. She used the word *resuscitation*.

I slid open our door. I am constitutionally incapable of minding my own business. I walked through the ICU on the premise of having to reach the bathroom. So many doctors and nurses had converged on the room at the end of the horseshoe that they spilled out the door. Outside the ICU, in the hallway, I passed a young, blank-faced priest in black clothes and white collar. He stopped to talk in Spanish to tearful men and women huddled by the ICU's double doors.

It wasn't until I was back in Ryan's room that I heard the mother. Her cry was flat and steady, a single sustained note, like the siren our town sounds when the creek waters are rising. I turned up the volume on Ryan's television. But I didn't need to. Almost immediately, the woman's cry grew fainter, but not in a way that suggested she had exhausted herself. She was leaving the ICU, moving away from us. I pictured her emerging from her child's room, walking through the ICU's automatic double doors and down the hallway, trailed by her grieving family. Maybe the priest was with them. Maybe he was still with the child, praying over the still body. I learned later the boy was twelve and had died of heart failure. I never saw him or his mother. I never knew what had made his heart stop.

The ICU was silent for a while. Then I heard a laugh from the nurses' station. Then several voices talked at once. A nurse slid our door open. I heard the other doors opening. Footsteps crisscrossed the floor. More laughter and more chatting.

Life goes on.

As horrible as I felt for the child and his family, I thanked God it wasn't Ryan and us. No matter how little Ryan might eventually recover, he was alive. I could hug him and kiss his head and squeeze his smooth hands. I already had been thinking about this several days earlier when I was getting my hair cut.

My longtime hairdresser, Simin, lost her eighteen-year-old son to suicide the previous January, eight months before Ryan's accident. We talked about him every month when I sat in the chair in front of her mirror.

She and her husband didn't know their son owned a rifle until they heard the blast from his downstairs bedroom. He was supposed to drive back the next day to UC–Davis, where he was a freshman. He had received his first-semester grades: straight A's. He was amazing. Everything seemed to come easy to Nima. He was smart, charismatic, funny. He had been student body president at Tamalpais High School in Mill Valley. He had competed on Tam's mock trial team, which won a national award. He played the piano. He performed in school plays and wrote poetry. He had a million friends.

He was the kid you never had to worry about.

On January 3, on his last day of winter break, Nima woke from a nap around 6:30 P.M. with a pounding headache. He was famished. He phoned in an order for takeout Chinese food, then he and Simin talked in the living room, waiting for Nima's father to return from work. Nima loved to talk, and Simin delighted in their conversations, though he could exhaust her with his ideas and thoughts, ricocheting from one topic to another, his mouth barely able to keep up with his brain.

At one point, Nima asked his mother if she could forgive him if he did something bad.

"What, you want to be a gangster?" she said.

Nima was always tossing out hypothetical situations for the sake of a good discussion, so the question didn't set off alarms.

"I'm going to do something that's going to hurt lots of people," he said.

His mother asked him what he meant. He didn't answer. Instead, he asked again if she would accept his decision even if she thought it shameful. She figured he was talking about doing something reckless and dangerous, like racing the Triumph motorcycle she and her husband recently bought for him.

"I am your mother, and you are my precious son," she told him. "Though I may not want to, in time, yes, I would accept."

By now, Nader, Nima's father, had returned home. Nima said he was going to pick up the Chinese food and went downstairs for the car keys. When they heard the blast a minute later, Nader ran outside. He thought Nima had crashed the car. Simin ran downstairs. She thought something had fallen on him.

Later the police found in the rifle case six typewritten notes to Nima's friends, brother, and parents. He had been planning this. He had everything ready. One note asked his best friend, Zach, to make sure he was buried with his peace-sign necklace and specified what music should be played at his memorial. Another gave permission to his friends at Davis to take whatever they wanted from his dorm room.

But none of the notes explained why Nima put a rifle in his mouth on a Tuesday night in January.

When I visited Simin and Nader after Nima's death, there was a poster-size photograph of their son over the white-brick fireplace. He was smiling his perfect smile. There were flower arrangements and plates of cookies and dates and strawberries. Simin had dark circles under her eyes. Nader looked worn.

"I'm sitting here trying to put every piece together," Simin said.

I had heard stories about Nima since he was a little boy, and I had met him once, when Simin had a grand opening party last year for her new salon in San Rafael.

She and Nader were tortured by the question that tortures so many parents of children who commit suicide: How could we not have seen? They had been scouring the volumes of poetry he wrote and the writings on his computer. They had been listening to every story from every friend and teacher. They were discovering a son they didn't know: a young man, it seemed, no one truly knew, who hid the darkest pieces of himself behind an exuberance and a competence beyond his years, which had made him one of the most popular students in high school.

Simin had since learned that the warning signs can look a lot like normal teenage angst: writings and drawings that refer to death, irrational behavior, changed eating or sleeping patterns. Everyone was looking back now, excavating clues from Nima's life: the painful breakup with his girlfriend last January, his disappointment about not being accepted to UC–Berkeley, the eleven hours a day he slept, the dark themes in his poetry.

The signs were there, maybe, if you knew exactly what to look for. But how do parents distinguish a seriously troubled teen from a dramatic, sensitive one?

Nader is an engineer whose job is to figure out where systems go wrong. Maybe, he said, sipping tea in his living room, Nima took too much to heart the complex teachings of the Koran and Rumi and other spiritual texts without the life experience to give him perspective. Maybe the virtual life that kids lead today—communicating through the Internet in language reduced to abbreviations—means their connection to other people, and to this world, is too light. Maybe parents are so busy making money for college tuition, and the kids are so busy making good grades, that families become loving strangers.

"Kids are involved in so many things that just seeing them in the morning and evening is an accomplishment," Simin said.

She had another theory, too, about Nima—one that was just as unknowable as any other. Maybe her son had a chemical imbalance that was never diagnosed.

Maybe, maybe, maybe.

John, Nima's older brother, was listening from a chair by the sliding glass doors as Simin and I talked.

"In every situation, we can look back and reconstruct the reality we want," he said. He was bothered that his parents seemed to be trying to reduce Nima's death to a single answer.

Nader nodded. "But we all need something to comfort ourselves," he said.

The room fell silent. Simin clutched a crumpled tissue, but she wasn't crying. She seemed cried out. At the memorial at the Mill Valley Community Center, she had sobbed quietly, burying her pained, shrouded face into the neck of every friend who hugged her. More than seven hundred people had come. They had filled every seat and sat on the floor in the center aisle and stood three and four deep along the walls. On a screen up front photos were flashed of Nima posing in his Batman costume as a little boy, playing in the snow at Tahoe, flashing a grin with his buddies at the prom.

I remember looking out the floor-to-ceiling windows of the community center. Two little girls in helmets rode past on pink bicycles. On the grass, a father tossed a football with his young son. The boy wrapped his arms around his father's waist, as if to tackle him. The father tried to run, and as they both tumbled, the father rolled onto his back to cushion his son's fall.

That's what you do, of course. That's what everybody does. You catch your kids. You protect them. You buckle them in, zip them up, warn them about strangers, slather on sunscreen, strap on elbow pads, tell them to wear their helmets. You do everything you can to keep them safe from the dangers of the outside world.

"We tried our best," Nader said, slumping deeper into the cushions of the living room couch. "We thought we knew Nima. But we're learning every day so many sides of him we didn't know. . . . We never worried for a second about suicide. Drugs, cars, alcohol, yes. Never suicide."

When anyone commented on how well I was holding up at the hospital day after day, week after week, I thought about Simin. She would have given anything to be in my shoes. So I considered every day at the hospital a gift: I still had my son.

Twenty-seven

After four days at UCSF, Ryan returned to Kentfield Rehab on Tuesday, October 10. The shunt was doing its job. The fluid had not returned. But Ryan was tired, mostly because of the pain in his left knee. No one could figure out what was going on. He couldn't straighten the leg anymore. The orthopedic doctor who examined him said the muscles around the knee had contracted, which can happen when people are bedridden for a long time. He ordered a brace that would, over time, stretch the muscles.

In the meantime, Ryan was reluctant to get out of bed and put any weight on the knee, but we made him sit in his wheelchair at least for meals, aiming for as much normalcy as possible in an abnormal environment. We lured him one evening into eating in the cafeteria for the first time with the bait of Clemania's chicken and rice. She had been telling Ryan about the dish for weeks and promised to make it for him when he could eat real food. Barry made pecan-crusted chicken, and I made cornbread, a favorite of Ryan's. We gathered around a linoleum-topped table and loaded our paper plates, Ryan in his wheelchair and helmet, listing slightly to the left even as he hunched over his food. When

In the Kentfield Rehab cafeteria for a feast with, from left, Dr. Bill Gonda, Barry, Lorna Stevens, Emma Stevens-Smith, Jesse Haskins (a former teacher of Ryan's), Ryan, and Clemania Felix, Ryan's nursing aide.

Ryan's pediatrician, Bill Gonda, showed up, and then one of his former teachers, Jesse Haskins, and then Lorna and Emma, we pulled another table over, handed out plates, and had a big, noisy family dinner.

It was not just Clemania who we now felt such a connection to, but the other parents and family members we saw every day in the hallways. After dinner, I saw Niki's mother, Cindy, retrieving some of Niki's things from her room. Niki had been taken to Marin General for a CT scan to see if she, like Ryan, had hydrocephalus. I stood with her at the door to Niki's room, and Cindy talked about trying to find the right doctor to reconstruct her daughter's face and how putting in a shunt was complicated by the fact that Niki had lost part of her skull and brain in the accident. Shared horror creates instant intimacy. We parents talked to each other in the hallways and parking lot about the most gruesome medical procedures as if we were sharing details of a dental filling.

Ryan was lucid in conversation, but his brain was still reconfiguring itself. His speech therapist gave him, for example, four numbers and asked him to repeat them backward. He couldn't hold the four numbers in his memory. But he could name the capital of the United States, the current president, the president before the current one, the number of states, a president who was assassinated, descriptions of Walt Disney, and Helen Keller. He couldn't come up with the capital of California or the name of the hurricane that hit the United States the previous year. He knew it had been in Louisiana, though.

"Given your current physical state," the therapist asked him, testing his logic, "how would you go to the grocery store to get food?"

"I'd ask my next-door neighbor to do it for me," Ryan said.

"You've got some good neighbors."

"I do."

"Well, what else could you do?"

"I could bring my next-door neighbor and drive him to the grocery store."

"Who's driving?"

"I am."

He was unable to take into account that he was in no condition to drive. He could not even *ride* in a car yet.

When the therapist pointed out these impediments to driving, Ryan had another answer.

"I could walk to my next-door neighbor's house and I'd sit in the car and wait for him to get the food."

Soon after moving into his new room at Kentfield, Ryan got another roommate, a lanky twenty-eight-year-old who had been at the rehab hospital for months. We weren't sure why he was moved in with Ryan, but we soon were thanking the powers-that-be. Brett fell almost immediately into the role of Ryan's big brother. He was soft-spoken and kind, quick to laugh, unfailingly cheerful. He had dropped out of college and had been working as a bartender when, late one summer morning, his twenty-four-year-old sister found him on the floor of their parents' Napa kitchen. He was blue and unconscious, and he had a gash on his head. A carton of vanilla ice cream was melting on the counter. No one knows how long he had been down. To this day, no one knows what happened. Brett couldn't remember anything about that morning or the night before. His parents had been on vacation in Idaho and rushed home.

Brett's brain injury slowed his speech, took away his short-term memory, and rendered his left foot almost useless. Months after his accident, he was still in a wheelchair, though he had been approved to leave the grounds with his family. His parents and sister took him out to lunch and dinner almost every week-end, driving down from Napa, but during the week he and Ryan kept each other company, grousing about the food or the grueling therapies, or speculating about the loud Wookie across the hall.

Barry took over blog duty one weekend. His entry made me laugh:

"There isn't a lot going on at the rehab center on the weekends, and we've felt Ryan could be getting a little too content to lie in bed instead of roust himself and cruise the halls in his wheelchair, so we've taken on the role of cruise director. Checkers in the cafeteria at 10 . . . a visit from Bill the dog on the terrace at 11:30 . . . *al fresco* grilled cheese on the back deck at 1 . . . specimen cup tossing at 4—that sort of thing.

"His spirits continue to be high although we think he's getting a little bit tired of the whole thing. He does have the surgery to put his bone flaps back coming up next week and we think that may be weighing on his mind a bit.

"His knee and his toes are a constant source of misery and trying to get an MRI scheduled to find out what is going on has been our constant source of misery.

"The MRI was set for tomorrow, but yesterday the head nurse—a lovely woman who last smiled when Coolidge was president—

told us that it had been cancelled because Ryan can't be near a magnet with the shunt that was put in last week. Of course everyone else had told us that it's OK. So now we're three weeks into trying to have the knee and toes diagnosed and we're no closer than we were at the beginning. Meanwhile his physical therapy is being hampered because he can't put weight on his left leg.

"With it all, he maintains the sense of humor that has made him the most popular guy in the place. I tell him everyday he's my hero—and he is.

"Please join us for bed-pan bowling in the halls at 6."

But the next day Ryan hit bottom.

I found him curled in bed when I arrived in the morning. His eyes were red. Barry had left town for a football game.

"What's the matter, sweetie?"

"I want to be home," he said. He turned his head into his pillow and cried as hard as he had since his accident. I started crying, too. I hugged him and said we would do what we could.

I persuaded the head nurse, then Dr. Doherty, for permission to take Ryan outside the hospital. They gave me instructions on what to do if he had a seizure (lay him on his side, keep everything out of his mouth, call 911). They made sure we knew we couldn't take him in a car because we had not been trained in transfers yet. They said we must have a nurse's aide with us at all times, that Ryan must wear his helmet, that he could not drink liquids. Okay, okay, okay, I said, hurrying to sign all the necessary papers.

It had been two months to the day that Ryan had been away from home.

Lucky for us, Tim was working that morning as Ryan's sitter. Tim was a tall, strong, easygoing guy who loved getting out of the hospital. At around 10:00 A.M., Tim and I wheeled Ryan— wearing a new dark blue helmet and loose sweats—through the parking lot of the rehab center, onto the paved bike trail, past the Ross tennis courts, through the parking lot of the post office, and into downtown Ross. Downtown is a half-block of small shops, including Café Marmalade and Eddie's, the corner grocery. Ryan wanted to stop and visit with everyone.

Debbie at Eddie's gushed, giving Ryan a hug and telling him how great it was to see him. I had noticed, though, a flicker of shock cross her face. I suddenly saw Ryan through the eyes of people who had not seen him since the accident. He was almost fifty pounds lighter. His face was gaunt and impassive, his eyes flat. And he was in a wheelchair wearing a helmet. He looked like someone whose life had been destroyed, someone whose appearance suddenly lowered the decibel level of any conversation. I wanted to hang a sign around his neck that made clear this was temporary, that he was not disabled. He was not brain damaged. He was not pitiable. He was going to be fine.

We rolled down Redwood to Brookwood and through our side gate. To the immediate left is the door to the garage. Ryan wanted to go in and see all his tools. We hadn't moved anything since his accident. Satisfied that all was well with his beloved saws and drills, he let Tim pull him in the wheelchair backward over the threshold and into the house (we were still learning the physics of maneuvering the wheelchair and now knew to go backward over bumps and down ramps). Inside, Ryan draped his arm around Tim's shoulder to rise from his chair and plop down on the couch. While he happily watched a rerun of *Roseanne*, I fetched his boa constrictor, Frankie, then his bearded dragon, Ozzie, thankful that we had managed to keep both alive while Ryan had been away.

I snapped pictures as I had been doing throughout Ryan's recovery, marking each milestone. Ryan was oblivious. He wanted a grilled cheese sandwich. And he watched the entire episode of *Roseanne*, the longest he had managed to stay focused on a single activity since the accident. For the next hour, he barely said a word. He looked completely content. His knee and foot didn't seem to bother him. But he had therapies starting at noon, so we had to get him back. On the way back, in front of Café Marmalade, we ran into Officer Bob, a longtime Ross police officer who had responded to Ryan's accident that August afternoon. He had known Ryan since kindergarten.

"Hey, buddy! Lookin' good," he said. Ryan shook his hand.

"I thought you'd be home that night," Officer Bob said. "I almost broke down when I found out the next day."

The trip home seemed to wipe Ryan out for the rest of the day. Maybe it simply was the physical exertion. Maybe going home and then returning to the antiseptic halls of the hospital made his sadness worse. Maybe he was worried about his bone-flap surgery on Wednesday. This would be the first surgery that Ryan knew was happening. He sometimes took the hand of visitors and guided it to the soft part of his head so they could feel it. I wondered if the gesture suggested he was still trying to make sense of what had happened to him.

"The good thing about getting your bone flaps back on, Ry," I said, "is you won't have to wear your helmet every time you get out of bed."

Ryan considered this for a moment.

"I'm still going to wear it," he said. "Just to be safe."

Twenty-eight

The morning before his surgery, on Tuesday, October 17, an ambulance once again carried Ryan and me across the Golden Gate Bridge, up Nineteenth Avenue to Parnassus and into the covered ambulance parking at UCSF. Familiar turf.

They rolled Ryan in the gurney to an enormous room at the end of a hallway on the sixth floor. He seemed to be the oldest kid on the floor by about thirteen years. I saw cribs in every room. There was even one across the room from Ryan's bed. The baby inside the crib, I learned later, was plagued by seizures. Her parents stood together at the crib, leaning over the rail to stroke her and talk softly to her. She was moved thirty minutes later to a room closer to the nurses' station, where she could be monitored more closely.

Ryan was on the standby list that day for an MRI of his knee and feet. He would need anesthesia to keep him still for the scan, so he had not been allowed to eat since the previous night. We waited through the morning. Then through lunch. The hang-up was not the availability of an MRI machine but getting an anesthesia team. Everyone was booked, so we'd get in only if a surgery was canceled.

When the nurse left the room, I gave Ryan a few sips of still-forbidden water as consolation for having no food.

We waited through the afternoon. No MRI. By 5:30, Ryan was in tears from hunger. We tracked down the nurse to find out the odds of the anesthesia team being available in the next hour. She reported back: there were still two kidney operations ahead of us. That was enough for us. Forget the MRI.

Barry went down to the cafeteria and returned with a hamburger and fries. And Lorna happened to show up just then with butterscotch pudding. Ryan looked like his old self, wolfing down the chow.

The nurse said Ryan would be back on the anesthesia/MRI waiting list for Friday, two days after his surgery.

Later Barry and I stood in the hallway and talked with Dr. Gupta, the neurosurgeon, about the following morning's surgery. He said it likely would last from 8:00 in the morning to 1:30 or 2:00 in the afternoon. The tedious part was peeling the scalp off the brain without causing too much bleeding. He explained also that often the bones don't fit back together perfectly, so there might be some dips or depressions in the skull. They wouldn't show up right away because the scalp would be swollen.

"But the biggest issue with the skin is closing it," he said. He would have to stretch the scalp to fit back over the bones. The scars, he said, might be fairly wide as a result. Hair doesn't grow on scar tissue, but in six months to a year, Ryan could have plastic surgery to narrow the scars and pull the hair together over them.

Gupta said Ryan likely would sleep the rest of the day after the surgery, and he probably would be sore and puffy for a day or two. He said he would like Ryan to stay at UCSF through the weekend.

Back in the room, I asked Ryan how he was feeling about the surgery.

"They've done a lot of these?" he asked.

"A million," I said.

"Okay."

That was it.

The surgery on Wednesday lasted five hours.

When Gupta unwrapped the bone flaps, he found the right side had a small defect, which had been patched at Marin General after the craniectomy with three titanium miniplates. There was another titanium miniplate holding together the original fracture, also on the right bone flap. Fitting the right and left bone flaps back onto the rest of the skull took another seven miniplates.

Ryan awoke from the surgery in late afternoon. His head was wrapped in white gauze. His face looked as if it had been pumped with helium. His eyes, swollen shut, were two thin slits. His body, by contrast, seemed even thinner and longer. He looked like a lollipop.

He opened his mouth to speak.

"Let's go home," he whispered.

I sat at his bedside through the night. Barry went home to take care of Bill and get some sleep so that he could take over in the morning. It was the first night I had spent in the hospital. It was the first time Ryan was cognizant enough, at least in ICU, to miss us.

"If your eyes stay shut for more than a day, I'll get you a seeing-eye dog," Barry joked. Ryan snorted out a laugh. He never asked for morphine, though he was hooked to a drip. When we or the nurses asked if anything hurt, he had the same answer: "My toes!"

Gupta came by on Friday to cut the bandages off Ryan's head. His skull looked smooth and round; from the swelling, Gupta said. He likely will have ruts where the bones didn't fit together perfectly and had to be glued, he said. There were strips of yellow tape in the shape of a McDonald's arch stretching from his forehead to the crown of his head. This was where Gupta sliced open the scalp, pulled the skin flaps back to reinsert the bones, then stitched them back together again.

Dr. Gupta assured us the swelling would soon subside, and, in fact, Ryan had thus far been a marvel in the speed of his recovery.

"When I looked at those CT scans when he first came to the ICU, I never dreamed he'd come this far this quickly," he said.

"You didn't realize who you were dealing with," Barry said.

Ryan went up for a CT scan around noon, then—*finally*—his MRI around 1:45. He had anesthesia for the MRI, so he had to stay in the recovery room for a while. Barry and I were sitting in Ryan's room reading the paper when Gupta appeared in the door.

The CT scan showed bleeding on the right side—the site of the original injury—between the dura and the scalp. The dura is the membrane that covers the brain. When the skull bones were taken out, Ryan's scalp had to be laid directly on the dura. The two layers inevitably ended up sticking to each other. During surgery to replace the bones, Gupta had to peel the scalp away from the dura, leaving the dura raw and oozy. That almost certainly was the source of the blood, Gupta said.

The blood showed up only on the right side. That was because, Gupta explained, the original blow to Ryan's brain had caused part of the brain to die off and shrink. The brain did not fill out the skull on the right side, which meant the skull exerted no pressure on the dura to stop the bleeding. The gap left from the atrophied portion of the brain allowed room for the blood to accumulate.

Gupta said Ryan would have another CT scan the next day, Saturday. If the bleeding continued, he would drill into the skull and drain it. But he hoped the blood simply would be reabsorbed.

Barry and I nodded and drove home without the radio and without a word passing between us. Our own brains, I think, had no room left for the prospect of another setback. I had never thought of Ryan's accident and complications as unfair. I never asked, Why us? Bad stuff happens. But during the silent ride home, I thought: Enough already. Ryan was done. He could not go through one more awful thing. His turn was over.

The CT scan Saturday morning showed the bleeding had worsened.

Barry had a football game in Berkeley. I was at UCSF by my-self when Dr. Peter Sun broke the news. He was the head of pedi-atric neurosurgery at Children's Hospital in Oakland and on the clinical faculty at UCSF. He was filling in for Dr. Gupta, who was away for the weekend at a conference.

There were two subdural hemorrhages, one under each flap, Dr. Sun told me. The one on the left was small enough to be of little concern. But the right had grown to the size of a bar of soap, Dr. Sun said. Worse, it was shoving the brain to the left, pushing it 7 mm off midline, the way the original swelling had done two months earlier. The right ventricle again was pinched shut. Dr. Sun said he had already consulted by phone with Dr. Gupta, who had called up the CT scan on his laptop. They both agreed Ryan needed surgery.

Christ.

Dr. Sun said the bleed was too large to be drained through a hole. He would have to remove the right bone flap that had been reattached just two days earlier.

My throat constricted. I felt tears welling. I didn't want to call Barry. There was nothing he could do even if he abandoned his game and rushed over. Let him work, have a few hours of respite. I would tell him after the game, when the surgery was over.

I signed the consent forms and stepped back into Ryan's room.

His eyes were still swollen shut. He was curled on his left side in a tight ball, as if warding off the hands and needles and tiny flashlights and IVs that seemed to be swarming him day and night.

I sank into a chair and cried, filling the wastebasket with Kleenex. My prized toughness, my self-sufficiency, cracked and fell to the tiled floor. I couldn't do this on my own. I knew Lorna was in an all-day website class. I called Erin and got her voice mail. I called Jill.

"I need you."

"Darling, I'll be right there."

Erin called back. "I'm getting in my car right now."

When they arrived about thirty minutes later, first Jill, then Erin, my throat was so tight I could barely speak.

"It's too much," I said. They hugged me hard, and Jill fetched another box of Kleenex from the nurses' station. Ryan was curled on his side in a fetal position, but he was awake. Erin kissed his swollen face. He said he had a headache. He asked for a pillow.

"Thank you, Erin," he said when she positioned it under his enormous head.

She knelt by his bed and covered his face again with soft kisses and whispered into his ear what a great kid he was and how the doctors were going to take good care of him. I blew my nose for the hundredth time, unable to stop the tears, leaning into Jill on the blue vinyl couch.

At noon, when the nurse said it was time, the three of us walked beside Ryan's gurney down the hall, into the elevator, and down to the fourth floor. We waited in the hallway for the anesthesiologist to take Ryan into the OR. I had draped Ryan's brown velour blanket over him. We all stroked his arms and legs and told him we'd be right there when he woke up.

"Are you warm enough?" I asked.

"I'm nice and warm," he said in a voice so sweet I had to walk away and cry some more.

Two hours later, when Dr. Sun walked through the doors of the ICU waiting room, he already was in street clothes with a backpack slung over his shoulder. He said everything went well. He removed the bone flap, suctioned out a fairly large volume of cerebrospinal fluid and blood, reattached the bone with more titanium miniplates, and stitched the dura to the skull by drilling holes in the bone. Ryan would have to lie flat to facilitate filling up the empty space where the spinal fluid and blood had been.

As Dr. Sun left, I heard from the hallway what sounded like a pulsing, whirring motor. I stuck my head out the door. An OR team was at the end of the hall, wheeling Ryan back toward ICU.

The strange sound was coming from Ryan's mouth. As the gurney got closer, the whirring became a wail, more animal than human. I pressed my hands against my face. How much more?

I followed Ryan and the OR team into Room 4, where he was rehooked to a half-dozen machines. Ryan's tongue was suspended and vibrating inside his open mouth like a baby in full cry. But Ryan's wail sounded as if it came from the deepest part of him, the one last part that had not been hurt, and now that, too, had been clawed at and ripped open. The moan, rising from his mouth in waves, seemed to say stop, stop, stop.

His head was huge, his eyes still bulging and sealed shut. I cried silently, determined not to add in any way to Ryan's misery. I flicked my fingertips under my eyes to clear the tears, but more tears took their place. I gave up and let them streak down my face.

I bent over Ryan and lightly ran my fingers down his arm to let him know I was there. He cried louder.

The anesthesiologist said the moaning probably was delirium from the drugs. He wasn't in actual pain, she said. She explained that because they had wheeled him straight from the OR to the ICU, we were seeing what is usually seen only in the recovery room.

I didn't believe any of it.

When the anesthesiologist left, Jill stomped out of the room and tracked down the ICU attending, a lovely Irish woman.

"He's in pain! He needs more medication!" Jill demanded.

The doctor agreed and upped his dose. It had no immediate effect. When a nurse tried to take blood, he lashed out, and Erin and I had to hold his arms. Jill swabbed his mouth with wet sponges. We soothed him the best we could, speaking softly, covering him with his soft brown blanket, all of us trying hard not to cry.

Lorna arrived at five, straight from her class, so Erin and Jill, having kept me going all day, finally could go home to their families.

When Barry called after the game in Berkeley, I told him about the surgery.

"I had a feeling," he said, letting out a heavy sigh. "How is he?"

By then, Ryan had stopped moaning. He was asleep from the morphine.

"He seems fine," I said. "They stopped the bleed. Everything seems to have gone the way it's supposed to, according to the doctor. His face is still a balloon."

"I'm on my way."

He arrived forty minutes later with Lorna's husband, Doug. Ryan was still sleeping. Barry kissed his enormous head.

"Bucky buck, I love you. You're the best kid in the world," he whispered.

We sat in his room for a while with Lorna and Doug. We spoke again with the nice Irish doctor. She would be there all night. She would make sure he wasn't in any pain.

We drove home telling ourselves what we always told ourselves: this is one day, and now it's over. Whatever tomorrow brings, we'll get through it, not because we're strong, but because there is no choice.

Twenty-nine

By the next day, the swelling in Ryan's face had begun to subside. Late in the afternoon, Ryan's right eye opened, just a slit. For the first time in four days, he could see us.

"How do I look?" Barry asked him.

"You look the same," Ryan said. He was quiet for a moment. Then: "It's disappointing."

Barry and I fell over laughing. His timing was perfect, his delivery deadpan (Okay, he couldn't move his facial muscles from the swelling, so deadpan was his only look. But still). It made our day.

When I arrived the next morning, Monday, Ryan was on his side with his back to the door. I bent down to kiss him and saw that he was crying.

"Sweetie, are you in pain?"

"No."

"What's the matter?"

"I don't have control over anything."

The neuro team—Gupta, interns, residents, and fellows—had just left. They must have been prodding and probing, checking his cognitive status, examining the stitches on his head, feeling for the shunt under his scalp, flexing his arms and legs. The patient has about as much say in the process as the dummy in CPR training.

As usual, Ryan almost immediately perked up, especially when Barry drew a big nose and a gap-toothed smile on the surgical mask I wore to prevent Ryan from getting my cold. He finally could open both eyes, and he watched Jim Carrey in *Liar, Liar* on TV.

Gupta sent Ryan back to Kentfield the next day, scheduling another CT scan to make sure the shunt was working and there were no more bleeds. At Kentfield, Ryan slept twenty-two of his first twenty-four hours. During the other two hours, he ate, the first real food in almost a week. He had lost another 10 pounds during his four days at UCSF, dropping him to a gaunt 160, nearly 60 pounds below his preaccident weight.

The hospitalization set back his physical therapy progress, too. His left side was weak again. The contracture in his left hamstring was even tighter, leaving his leg bent at the knee at about a 30-degree angle.

When he was awake, we passed the time playing Boggle and picking out a pool table for the garage. Barry had a catalog and showed Ryan a table with curved Queen Anne legs.

"Queen Anne," Ryan said, "must have had a pretty tough time walking."

Ryan's continued lethargy concerned Dr. Doherty at Kentfield. This was more than the aftereffects of his surgery. He should have rebounded by now, she said. She sent him to Marin General for a CT scan. A few hours later, I got a call on my cell phone from Eastham, Dr. Doom.

"He needs something done immediately," he said.

He was on rotation at Marin General that week. When he saw Ryan's name on the scan, he took a look. He said there was fluid pooling on both sides of the brain, more specifically between the brain and the skull. Right now, he said, Ryan's brain looked great, considering what he had been through. But if the buildup of fluid was left untreated, it could press on the brain and damage it.

If Ryan were still his patient, he said, he would insert a drain on each side immediately.

Shit. Shit. Shit. Shit.

I called Gupta at UCSF and Dr. Manley at SF General. Both disagreed with Eastham. They said the brain would likely reabsorb the fluid on its own. Drilling into the skull to insert drains posed greater risks than doing nothing, Manley said. Every time you expose the skull, you risk infection. He said one in five cranioplasties (the surgery Ryan just had to replace the bone flaps) results in the flaps becoming infected. The infected bones have to be thrown away and replaced by prosthetic segments. It is an awful experience to be avoided at all costs, Manley said.

Ryan, of course, not only had had the cranioplasty, but three days later his skull bone was removed yet again to drain a bleed. And he already had bur holes from two previous drains. So far he had been lucky.

"If we went in yet again to get the fluid in there now, he would be at a very high risk of infection," Manley said.

He and Gupta recommended waiting. Ryan would get another CT scan the following day to see if the fluid was accumulating, diminishing, or staying stable.

When I told Eastham that we decided against the drains, he could barely contain himself.

"There's no way at all this will go away on its own," he said. I could hear the alarm and frustration in his voice. He still felt such a stake in Ryan's recovery. He was like a starting pitcher who is afraid his relievers are about to blow a hard-fought game. He was convinced Gupta and Manley were making a dangerous mistake.

I hung up feeling sick. Were we doing the right thing? After all, Eastham had been right about the hydrocephalus.

Ryan's behavior did nothing to ease my worries. For the rest of the day, he was so lethargic he couldn't get through his therapies.

He kept falling asleep, and when he wasn't asleep, he was weepy and sensitive. Everything seemed to hurt. During speech therapy, when the therapist asked if he could work for fifteen more minutes, he broke into tears.

"I always say yes," he said. "But I don't think I have it in me."

Late that afternoon, he awoke crying.

"What's the matter?" I asked. "Did you have a bad dream?"

"I dreamt I had to bring somebody back from the past, and I couldn't get him." His face twisted in grief. "I failed."

"Did you need to bring him back to save him?" I asked.

"No," he said. "To save me."

The CT the next morning showed no change in the fluid buildup. It was Friday. We had an appointment with Gupta for Monday. After the CT and morning therapies, an aide and I wheeled Ryan home. Dr. Doherty allowed Ryan these short visits because the buildup of fluid wouldn't be better or worse whether he was in the hospital or at our house. I made grilled cheese for lunch while Ryan curled up under a blanket on the couch and laughed through *America's Funniest Home Videos*. I hadn't heard him laugh in days.

That evening, Clemania stopped in to say hello. I told her we had visited home.

"We did?" Ryan asked.

"You don't remember?" I couldn't believe it. I thought he must be joking.

"No."

"We had grilled cheese, remember? And watched *America's Funniest Videos?*"

"No, I don't remember."

I dropped it, fearing I might upset him.

A little while later, when he was in the bathroom with his aide, I heard him pounding, pounding, pounding on the wall and moaning.

"Ry, stop. What's the matter?" I asked, opening the door.

"I don't know."

"Are you angry about something?"

"Yes."

"What is it?"

"I don't know."

"You're just angry?"

"Yes."

Who could blame him? His anger was the sanest response to what he had been through.

Ryan had lunch at home again on Saturday, and at 7:00 Sunday morning the phone woke me. Ryan was crying.

"Mom!" Ryan said, sounding grief-stricken. "Come get me! I want to go home!"

I threw on clothes, rushed over, and found him already dressed and in his wheelchair. I wheeled him home, where I made him pancakes and bacon. He watched *The Fast and the Furious*. Throughout the day, visitors stopped by: Ryan's first-grade teacher, Mrs. Frank; Barry's ex-wife and her husband. Ryan's Kentfield roommate Brett and his parents came over for lunch. It was a lovely day, capped by Barry's return from a business trip in the late afternoon. I walked next to Ryan's chair as Barry pushed him down the bike trail back to the hospital.

"Pretty soon, you'll be walking on this trail," I said.

Ryan burst into tears.

"I don't think so," he said.

"You don't think you'll walk?" Barry asked.

"Yeah."

Barry assured him that he would. He said he would return to just how he was before the accident, that what he was going through was what almost all brain-injured people go through. We weren't sure he believed it. He clearly was harboring unspoken fears; it would explain the panic that so often gripped him.

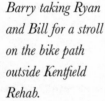

*Barry taking Ryan
and Bill for a stroll
on the bike path
outside Kentfield
Rehab.*

His memory was still failing him. His friend, Olivia, called him that night at the hospital. She had been calling regularly and had visited him several times at UCSF. She was just checking in.

"How are you doing?" she asked.

"Not so good," Ryan said, beginning to cry. "I'm in the hospital. I fell off my skateboard."

I knew memory lapses were typical of brain injuries. But maybe they were getting worse from the buildup of fluid. He would have another CT scan tomorrow and see Gupta. We would know more then.

But we didn't see Gupta the next day. He postponed the appointment and the CT until the following Monday, saying he wanted to put a little time between the scans to see if there was any change. Dr. Doherty at Kentfield, however, wasn't comfortable with waiting. She scheduled a CT scan at Marin General for the next day.

To lift Ryan's spirits, Barry decided to get burgers for lunch. As he drove through the Kentfield parking lot, he heard a crack, as if lightning had hit the roof of his car. He stepped on the brakes. In the next instant, the enormous iconic oak tree came crashing to the ground. Several tons of branches hurtled toward the car in a thunderous roar. Staffers and visitors poured out of the hospital to see the gigantic tree sprawled across the parking lot. One huge branch had crushed a wood-and-concrete railing along the edge of the lot.

Then they spotted the bumper of a car beneath the mountain of splintered wood. Someone called 911. Others rushed over, prepared for the worst. Just as they reached the tree, Barry was emerging, digging his way out from under the tangle of branches and leaves.

"Wow, how 'bout *that?*" he said to speechless onlookers.

Picture a wishbone with a third bone curving up and out from the joint. The tree had fallen so that the three largest branches landed around Barry's car like a cage. The two lower branches landed on either side of the car, and the curved branch arched over it. The car had to be in exactly the right spot to avoid being flattened like a tin can. It was like one of those Buster Keaton clips where the front wall of a house falls forward and Keaton is standing exactly where the door opening is, so he emerges unscathed.

"You ought to catch the first plane to Vegas," one hospital attendant said, clapping him on the back.

The fire department hacked and sawed for an hour to clear a path for our trapped car. When a firefighter backed the car out, there wasn't a scratch on it. Bartlett's Tree Service spent the rest of the week with chainsaws, pulleys, and motorized cherry pickers, cutting and hauling away the ancient tree limb by enormous limb. We never found out why it fell. There was no rain, no lightning.

Barry couldn't walk into Kentfield Rehab without staffers stopping to relive the whole miraculous episode. Barry laughed and shook his head appropriately, but he did not feel the way everyone seemed to expect him to feel: that he had cheated death and therefore should be either traumatized or in awe of his amazing luck. To him, and to me, the episode didn't seem particularly extraordinary. We had become accustomed to extraordinary. Extraordinary was our new normal.

Thirty

Ryan woke up crying again. He got his sitter to dial our phone.

"Mom," he said. "Where are you?"

"I'm on my way."

I didn't know exactly why he was crying. He was lonely. He was sad. He was confused. He was exhausted.

The sky was still dark when I jogged up the bike path to the hospital, then climbed into bed with him, wrapping him in my arms and kissing his lumpy head.

"Oh, baby," I whispered. "I'm here, sweetie-pie."

When he stopped crying, I helped him dress, pulled his knit cap down to his ears, and wheeled him down the bike path and across the street to Café Marmalade. We had scones and croissants, then decided to visit his old teachers at Ross School a half-block away. Everyone made a fuss. I could see them working hard not to wince or tear up at the sight of the wheelchair and bony legs and slight slump to the left. I worked hard not to cry at their genuine affection for Ryan. I spent all those years embarrassed and exasperated by his behavior at school, and what these teachers seemed to remember most about Ryan was his heart and his humor.

I thought about my brother Bobby, whose terminal cancer made him a sympathetic character for the first time. I was seeing that with Ryan, too. Kids who hadn't bothered with him in the past were visiting him in the hospital. Parents who had never been sure what to make of this clunky, prickly but bighearted child now were marveling at his courage and perseverance. Suddenly he was the most popular kid in town, a star wherever he went, folks eager to shake his hand and tell him how amazing he was. I wondered if, when Ryan was fully recovered, he would feel the kind of letdown Bobby did. If he was no longer injured, he was no longer special. He would just be Ryan again. Would he understand, even if others didn't, that he had always been a kid with courage and perseverance and humor, and that the accident merely highlighted those traits? Would he remember, when others forgot, that he was that amazing person, even when he no longer needed a wheelchair?

We returned to the hospital for physical therapy, and despite pain in his left foot and tightness in his hamstrings, Ryan walked between the parallel bars and briefly with a walker for the first time since he returned from UCSF. Then the therapist wheeled him to the parking lot, where he learned how to get in and out of our car. We were cleared to drive him to appointments—no more ambulances. I promptly drove him, with Tim, his aide, to Marin General for a CT scan. But the best part of the day was yet to come.

"Let's try a swallow test," the speech therapist said when she arrived in Ryan's room for his afternoon session.

I followed as she wheeled him into a small radiology room off the lobby. Ryan had to drink a white, chalky liquid that coated his lips and tasted so bad he cried. The radiologist watched the barium solution wend its way down Ryan's esophagus into his stomach.

Not a drop slipped into his lungs.

"You're cleared for water," the speech therapist announced.

Finally, finally, finally.

Ryan wheeled himself out the door, through the lobby, and straight to the cool metal water fountain that had tantalized him since arriving at Kentfield six weeks earlier. He leaned over the spout, turned the spigot, and drank. He stopped, took a breath, and drank some more. He made his way down the main hall and the side halls, stopping at every water fountain. He ended his tour in front of the vending machine in the cafeteria. I gave him a dollar, which he fed into the slot. He pushed the button and down rolled a can of root beer. He drank three.

We had pizza at home that night, Halloween. Ryan's roommate, Brett, and his tutor, Caroline, handed out candy with us. Then Erin and Rob stopped by with their youngest daughter, Tierney, dressed as a pirate. Emma showed up with four girlfriends. It felt like a celebration.

The CT scan showed no change in the buildup of fluid that had Eastham so worried. We couldn't figure out if that was good news or bad news. We would have to sit tight for another five days, until we saw Gupta at UCSF on Monday.

In the meantime, I tried to find ways to distract Ryan from the pain in his left foot. It was getting worse. We often could joke him out of his jags of pain and irritability, but sometimes he was inconsolable. So on Saturday, I helped Ryan into the car and took him to the movies to see *Flushed Away*. The theater was nearly empty, so we took two seats on the aisle. Ryan sat through the entire show, using the plastic urinal bottle right at his seat; luckily no one was sitting within eye- or earshot.

We spent the rest of the weekend living the closest thing we had to a normal life in more than two months. We went to a high school soccer game to watch one of Ryan's friends. When the team won in double overtime Ryan joined the fans at midfield in his wheelchair for the celebration. We went to another movie and had take-out Chinese food at home.

We arrived early for our appointment the next morning with Gupta at UCSF. Ryan needed to use the bathroom. Barry took him in, and when they emerged, Ryan was beaming.

"Mom!" Ryan said. "Guess what I just did? Dad, tell her."

In the bathroom, as Barry was locking the wheelchair's wheels in preparation for helping Ryan up, Ryan stood up on his own, without holding on to Barry or to a railing or anything. Just stood up perfectly, as if he had forgotten he was not supposed to be able to do that yet.

"Wow! You won't need us for anything pretty soon," I said.

When we were summoned into the office, Gupta was smiling. The CT scan showed that 80 percent of the fluid had been reabsorbed, just as he and Manley had predicted. No need for drains. No adjustment to the shunt. No nothing. Dr. Eastham had told me that he would eat his hat if the fluid disappeared on its own. We thought about presenting him with a Yankees cap.

We bragged to Gupta that Ryan had just stood on his own, prompting Ryan to unbuckle his seatbelt and rise from his chair.

"Wow," Gupta said. "You're tall! I've never seen you out of bed before!"

The three of us were almost giddy as we left the office. We stopped on Geary Street for a celebratory lunch. As we drove back across the Golden Gate Bridge, Barry and I talked about finding a gym where Ryan could keep building up his muscles after he left Kentfield. We debated the merits of various gyms according to the classes and sports they offered.

Ryan interrupted.

"It'd be nice to walk first," he said.

Barry and I laughed. He was right. We were getting ahead of ourselves. I reminded myself: *Today, today, today.*

In the car that day, in the time it took to drive from the city to Marin, I could see Ryan awakening, moving closer to his old self. He was singing along with the radio, something he hadn't done since his accident. We were listening to a classic rock station. The BeeGees launched into "Stayin' Alive." Ryan raised his arms and started dancing in his seat the way he used to do.

"Da-Da-Da-Da-stayin' alive, stayin' alive, . . ." he sang.

How he knew the words, I had no idea. But he was rocking out, singing and laughing and waving his arms over his head. Barry and I joined in, and soon we all were singing at the top of our lungs. (My sister Donna, reading of this on my blog, had no comment on Ryan's progress but wanted to know why in God's name we were listening to the BeeGees.)

I felt almost ecstatic, like my son was back—not yet completely, I knew, but his spirit had returned, it seemed, and that was everything.

Half a year before Ryan's accident, I had signed up to attend the Nieman Narrative Conference, which was to be held the weekend of November 17 in Boston. I had decided the previous spring to suspend my column so I could write longer, more complex pieces, such as the five-part series about Iraq War veterans that won the White House Correspondents' top award in April. The conference had become, in my mind, the portal through which I would arrive at the next phase of my career. I wanted to write ambitious, literary stories, and the Nieman conference was an opportunity to learn from the best writers and editors in the country. I had been looking forward to it for months.

Barry had to be out of town the same weekend, so my parents agreed to watch over Ryan while we were away. They flew in on Monday, November 13, loaded down with gifts from my brothers and sisters. Ryan loved everything, and he fell happily into the teasing and kidding that passed between my parents and him like lines from an old movie.

There wasn't much for them to worry about. Ryan hadn't had any seizures, but I told them what to do just in case he had one while he was with them. All they had to do was keep him company at Kentfield Rehab. Everything was set.

"It will do you good to get away," my mother said.

But the morning after my parents arrived, two days before I was to leave for Boston, I woke up with the realization that I could not get on the airplane. I couldn't leave Ryan. I wasn't ready.

I can't identify what I was feeling exactly. It was something I had never known, at least not with such intensity.

I had left Ryan many times before. I remember when Ryan was six years old and I flew off to Atlanta for the 1996 Olympic Games. I relished the thought of a hotel room to myself, of eating when I wanted, of immersing myself in work without calls from the principal or meltdowns on play dates. I remember feeling a little guilty for how much I enjoyed getting away for two weeks.

This time, it wasn't about whether Ryan needed me. I needed Ryan. I had never needed anybody—truly, absolutely needed anybody, not even Barry. This was something else, something elemental, like needing food and water.

Later that week, when I should have been in Boston, I lingered outside the physical therapy room instead, watching my son. He stood at the start of the parallel bars, supporting himself with a hand on each bar. Hans, his therapist, stood a few feet in front of him, encouraging him to let go of the bars and take a step. Hans was close enough to catch him if he stumbled. Ryan released his grip, keeping his hands hovering over the bars, just in case. He took a step. Then another. His hands dropped to his sides.

He walked the entire length of the parallel bars without touching them.

At the end, he broke into a big smile, raised his arms, and shook his body in a goofy little dance. I clapped from the hallway.

Thirty-one

I turned a corner one day at Kentfield to find myself walking behind a man accompanied by two armed correctional officers. He was shuffling, hampered by the steel cuffs on his ankles. He was an inmate from San Quentin State Prison, up the road just three or four miles. This was where the prisoners came for rehab. Death-row inmates, I learned, had three guards; the regular guys had two. There always seemed to be at least one inmate in residence.

"How's it going?" I said, passing him on the left.

"Okay. You?"

"Great."

What a weird little world we had landed in. A girl with half her head missing; a man strapped into a wheelchair moaning for his mother day and night; killers taking their morning constitutional in the company of armed guards; a kind and funny young man still trying to figure out how he ended up unconscious on the kitchen floor with a brain injury so severe he might never walk as smoothly or think as sharply again; a middle-aged woman so disoriented from strokes she believed she was just stopping by the rehab hospital for a ladies' lunch; an ER doc paralyzed from

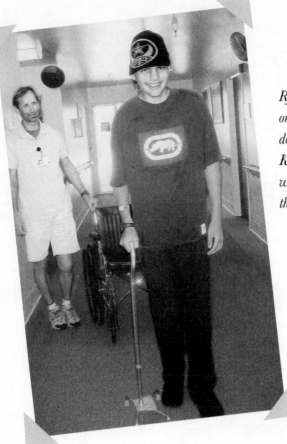

*Ryan walking
on his own
down the hall of
Kentfield Rehab
with his physical
therapist, Hans.*

the waist down from a Range Rover slamming into him and his bicycle; a mute and blank-eyed young man staring from his bed at his exhausted mother.

And in the midst of all this, Ryan.

He was getting stronger every day, moving with confidence as he got in and out of his wheelchair. He was walking on his stick-thin legs for longer periods with a walker or a cane, though the effort exhausted him. In the afternoons, when his therapies were over, he was always ready to go home. He even began climbing the stairs up to his bedroom, leaning heavily on the railing, to visit with Ozzie, Frankie, and Cheeto (his bearded dragon, boa constrictor, and leopard gecko). Mostly, though, he'd flop on the living room couch and watch *Roseanne* reruns and eat grilled cheese sandwiches. I'd cover him with a blanket, then plop down on the loveseat next to him with my own blanket, and we'd watch TV until dark. I'd wheel him back on the bike trail, following the circle of white light from the flashlight in Ryan's hand.

At home at night, I opened statements from my insurance company. Two or three arrived every day. By early November, the stack had grown to about four inches high. My rough calculation had the total bill so far at about $1.5 million, not counting the rehab hospital.

"What's your lifetime limit?" a friend asked one day.

"Lifetime limit?"

We might be responsible for anything over, say, $1 million, she said. My stomach dropped. So far our copays had added up to less than $2,000, so the financial part of all this had barely crossed our minds. I immediately called the insurance company.

"Let me see," said the representative on the phone. "No. No lifetime limit."

ThankyouGod.

Dr. Doherty said Ryan likely would be cleared to return home the following Tuesday, almost a week away. We decided to push for Friday. He had no therapies scheduled for the weekend, so why wait? We met with Dr. Doherty and Ryan's therapists in a conference room off the lobby.

"We don't have to tell you how far he's come," Dr. Doherty said, peering over her glasses at us. "He came from a pretty dicey place."

One by one, the therapists delivered status reports.

The physical therapist said Ryan still needed a wheelchair to cover anything but the shortest distances. He still needed someone to stand next to him when he was upright. His leg muscles were still contracted and painful. He had balance issues. He was impulsive.

The speech therapist said he had regained some intonation—

he wasn't as robotic in his speech. He still struggled with inflexible thinking. He had a very short attention span. He had gotten better at asking for instructions to be repeated rather than blundering through. He was less egocentric. He still had poor judgment. He needed lots of supervision.

His occupational therapist said his progress had been amazing. He was dressing himself, brushing his teeth, washing his face, all on his own. But he was so impulsive that he had to be monitored constantly.

Dr. Doherty listened until they were finished. She pursed her lips and removed her glasses.

"He's had a serious injury to the part of the brain that regulates emotions and judgment," she said. "Add to that the fact that the frontal lobe is not fully developed until the age of twenty-five. He is at risk for serious problems with safety and judgment."

She wanted to make sure we were fully aware of the responsibility we were about to take on. Ryan's confidence put him in danger of doing something stupid. He had to be watched. Structure is critical, she said. His day must be predictable. He needed lots of sleep; lack of sleep can trigger seizures. He could die if he drinks alcohol. He cannot drive. He cannot ride a bike, a skateboard, or a snowboard for a year. She listed the medications he needed to take and when.

Yes, yes, yes, yes, we said. Where do we sign?

On a mid-November Saturday, ninety-four days after his fall from a skateboard on Lagunitas Road, Ryan returned home. Barry was away on business, so my parents and I stuffed Ryan's clothes, books, DVDs, leg braces, photographs, and get-well cards into white plastic hospital bags.

Clemania came by to hug Ryan and kiss his face and make him promise to visit. Tim came by, and Hans. Darlene, the mother of Josh, who was still unable to speak or get out of bed, hugged me and wished us good luck. I hugged her back and told her I had come to believe in miracles.

When we drove up to the house, an enormous hand-painted sign from Erin and her three kids hung across our two-car garage: "Welcome Home, Ryan!" Balloons swayed in the breeze at the ends of ribbons tied to the maple tree by the back gate.

"Look, Ryan! Isn't that nice?"

He barely noticed. He already was unfastening his seatbelt.

"Wait! Let me get the chair!" I said, watching him open the door and swing his legs out.

He wanted to go directly into the garage to play video games, but I coaxed him into going into the house first. Inside, Jill and her daughter Ellie waited with a sheet cake and more balloons.

"Ryan! You're home!" Jill said, beaming and wrapping him in a big hug.

"Thanks," Ryan said, hugging her back but already looking exhausted. He asked if he could go into the garage now.

"Sure."

I had the sense that after waiting so long to return home, he wasn't absorbing the fact that it was happening. Or maybe he just wanted to slip back into his old life, erasing the last three months from his memory. The truth was he remembered almost none of the three months, including his early days at Kentfield Rehab. Just as well.

Friends stopped in throughout the day as word spread that Ryan was home. That night, Ryan and I burrowed under the covers in my bed, watching a movie until he started to nod off.

"Time for bed, sweetie," I said, shaking him gently and kissing his forehead.

I followed him as he walked with his cane down the short hall into his own room and his own bed.

The white down comforter had not been turned down since the night of his accident. Now Ryan lifted it and the pale green top sheet and slid under them, pulling them over him in a single motion. He smiled and sighed. I switched off the lamp by his bed.

"Good night, Mommy-mom."

I bent and kissed his forehead.

"Good night, baby-babe. I love you."

"I love you, too. You're the best mom in the world."

"You're the best kid in the world."

Ryan turned on his side and burrowed into his pillow. He pulled the comforter up over his shoulders and clutched it under his chin. I stood in the dark doorway, listening to him breathe.

Bill hopped onto the bed and curled up at Ryan's feet.

Thirty-two

Within a week, Ryan was rarely using the wheelchair, mostly out of pity for me. I was pushing him one day down Redwood Avenue on our way home from Café Marmalade. I had Bill on a leash, and I was holding a latte. Then my phone rang. To answer it, I had to steer with my elbows, and suddenly the wheelchair was turning this way and that in the middle of the street. We both were laughing when we heard a thunderous pounding. We looked up to see a stampede of about a hundred kids bearing down on us. It was the annual Ross School Turkey Trot, and we were smack in the middle of the route. Ryan and I laughed so hard at the absurdity of the scene that we almost peed our pants.

The next day, we bought a camouflage-colored cane at Jack's Drug Store in San Anselmo, cooler-looking than the hospital-issue cane—and the wheelchair went in the garage.

We cooked big dinners almost every night that winter, crowding our kitchen table with friends who had protected and carried us.

I made the humbling discovery that in stepping away for three months, the newspaper world continued perfectly well without me. The *Chronicle* still landed on people's doorsteps every morning, the pages filled with columns and stories that weren't mine. For nearly a quarter of a century, I was a newspaper columnist. It was a dream job but came with the unrelenting stress of generating multiple columns a week and weathering the equally unrelenting public critiques. *I didn't have to keep doing it.* Eight months after Ryan returned home, I volunteered for a buyout as the *Chronicle* downsized.

During those first months at home, I saw changes in Ryan that I had not noticed in the hospital. For example, he was as egocentric as a five-year-old; he related everything to himself. If he saw someone boxing on television, he would remark on how he would box differently, never mind that he had never boxed. If he saw an interesting building, he would explain how he could build something similar. One of his therapists at the outpatient center at Kentfield Rehab, where Ryan went for therapy every day, said he was moving through the stages of child development all over again. He's like a child who sees himself as the center of the universe. He would move beyond it as his brain healed.

His current self, she explained, was born when the accident happened.

So, I knew, was mine.

We saw evidence almost every day of Ryan's healing. He was speaking more clearly. He was able to remember details of short stories. But he was as distractible as a puppy. I sat in on a session when his speech therapist read a paragraph about cucumber soup in order to test his comprehension.

"I hate cucumbers," Ryan said, interrupting. He pried his right shoe off from the heel, pulled the foot onto his left knee, and rubbed. "I hate cold soup. I cannot have cold soup. It's like having warm milk. That's disgusting."

"Okay, Ryan," the therapist said, moving on. "What do you call the thing you use to tie your shoes?"

"I wear slip-ons," Ryan said. "And they're fuzzy inside, too." He lifted his shoe to show her.

"What is the difference between a pen and a pencil?" the therapist asked.

"One uses ink and one uses lead," Ryan said. "Well, actually graphite. But I still have lead pencils, which is really, really odd. My grandfather was an architect, and he had lead pencils with real lead inside." He then described how the mechanical pencil worked.

Despite diminished short-term memory and profoundly slow processing speed, Ryan returned to school part-time in January 2007, five months after his accident. He took English, photography, and art, and we hired a tutor to teach him world history that summer so he could earn enough credits to be a junior in the fall.

One day, a few months after he returned home, he was playing pool in the garage with Barry. Jack Johnson was playing through the speakers of his iPod. (Jack Johnson's music was on for hours a day in Ryan's room while he was in his coma.)

"Dad, I know I've never heard this song and I know all the words," he said.

If the music had seeped into his comatose brain, I figured our voices had, too. He must have heard us telling him that he would be okay, that he couldn't die, that we could not survive that.

Ryan doesn't remember the ambulance, the emergency room, the coma, or much of anything during the ninety-four days he spent in three different hospitals. My tower of latte cups, each marked with an hour and date, had no meaning for him. I had saved them during those first days at Marin General, when I kept expecting him to wake up so I could fetch his clothes from the backseat of the car. I thought, back then, we were in the midst of something that could be measured in paper cups.

Though Ryan remembers nothing of the accident, the story of the fall has taken root in his memory from what we have recounted to him. He would tell people he remembered wobbling on his skateboard just before he fell. He would give details. His brain deleted the actual experience. So did mine, to some extent.

The three months my son spent in hospitals now seem like windows on a passing train. I catch glimpses of myself in the blue vinyl chair inside his ICU room, at the computer screen looking at a CT scan with the neurosurgeon, in the waiting room accepting another latte from Lorna, at the side of my son's bed coaxing him to squeeze my fingers.

But if some of the details of the experience have fluttered from my mind, the experience itself has not. It changed me, as such experiences do. You always hear that. One moment your life is one way, then suddenly it is something else, and you, more or less, have become someone else. But, of course, the change isn't as sudden as all that. It's not like walking through a door. It's more like erosion, when the elements buffet and pound and scrape a thing until it has changed shape. It is not something completely new— it is still that same thing—but it has different angles and crevices, a different orientation to, and role in, its surroundings.

That's what happened to me. I wonder if just as Ryan's brain was altered by the accident, mine was, too. Did the experience make me softer and more affectionate, or did it reveal qualities that had simply been buried? Did some rewiring take place that had me perceiving stimuli and processing information in a different way? That allowed me to let go of control, to be accepting and patient, to realize what I can and cannot fix?

For ninety-four days in 2006, my life hurtled backward, then slowly forward again. I got a second chance. A do-over. It came at an enormous price that I would not have chosen. But I shiver to think that I might have gone through the rest of my life as the mother I was, as someone who never saw her son for who he is. Is it selfish to be thankful for something so horrible?

When I sat down to write this book, I couldn't find my notebooks. I had taken notes almost every day of Ryan's hospitalization. Much of it ended up in the blog I wrote on CaringBridge.org, but some of it didn't. I tore the house apart. Scoured the garage and shed and both cars. Nothing. They were gone, perhaps tossed out with the recycling. I had never lost a notebook in twenty-five years as a journalist, and now I had lost all three that chronicled my son's injury and recovery.

"Do you really think it's an accident that you lost the details of the most awful time of your life?" my friend Toni asked.

At first, I was physically ill, of course, and lay awake at night examining in my mind every corner and cabinet in every room of the house. But soon I found that when I told someone about the lost notebooks, I was shrugging.

It is what it is.

I would have to take a different approach to writing the story. I ordered all of Ryan's medical records and spent weeks reading and organizing them. I went back and interviewed all his doctors. I interviewed my friends for all their recollections. Like Ryan, I had to figure out ways to fill in the gaps, rely on different skills, work harder.

The accident had seemed at times like the relentless advance of a forest fire, out of control, leveling our lives. Now we were seeing, of course, the gift in the destruction. You get to see your life pared to its elemental needs: food, water, community, love. To my own list, I add redemption.

Thirty-three

One day in the fall of 2007, after Ryan had returned to school full-time, he asked me to help him with a one-page essay on Lincoln's plan for reconstruction. We had two wonderful tutors, but school was still a struggle. Ryan is likely to have short-term memory deficits and slow processing for the rest of his life. He had failed his first two chemistry tests, even with the benefit of open notes. We reminded Ryan that all he had control over was how hard he worked. He couldn't control the results of his work. If he failed every test all semester, so be it. The teacher began testing Ryan orally, and his results improved enough to pass the class.

We took the long view. Ryan was in high school not to prepare him for more schooling, though we fully expected him to go to college. He was in high school to prepare him for the rest of his life. We were more concerned about him learning perseverance than the periodic table. We were more concerned about him learning self-reliance than *The Scarlet Letter*.

I rarely looked at his grades. They didn't matter. The progress I wanted to see was in self-confidence, in the ability to research and organize, the willingness to try again when he failed, the ability to control his temper and frustration when he didn't understand something or felt overwhelmed. (Sudden rages are a common problem in the aftermath of a brain injury, and we have the gouged walls, shattered mirrors, and broken chairs to prove it. His psychiatrist eventually put Ryan on Abilify, which helped tremendously but led to weight gain. We're now grappling with finding an alternative that won't interfere with his seizure meds and Adderall.)

For the first six weeks of school, Ryan could barely get through a page from his history or English books without a tutor or Barry or me by his side, reading along, going over the questions at the end of the chapters, guiding him through every step. Bit by bit, week by week, we pulled back.

So when he asked for help on his Lincoln question, I told him, "You really can do this on your own. You don't need me."

"I know," he said. "But I like you here. I do better when you're in the room."

"Sure," I said.

I picked up a paperback and propped a pillow behind me on the trundle bed in the upstairs room where Ryan did his homework. He bent over his history textbook, running a yellow highlighter over lines of type. His brow furrowed as he puzzled through a particular passage. Next to the desk stood a tall, narrow baker's rack we used as a bookshelf. Ryan and I had found it in an antique store the summer before his accident. He always looked for the most unusual items, saying that a thing was most valuable when there was no other like it.

I looked at him with his back to me, bent over his history book. He was amazing, remarkable, courageous, gracious. My throat constricted. My eyes fell on the black three-ring binders on a bottom shelf, the ones I filled throughout his childhood with school evaluations, special-ed forms, and articles on ADD, pieces of the puzzle I was determined to solve.

They seem as if from somebody else's life.

I rose from the trundle bed and crossed the room. I stood behind Ryan and rested one hand on his shoulder and ran the other over the rough topography of his reconstructed skull, the crevices and bumps, the dips and mounds, the ropey scars under his buzz cut. Then I bent and pressed a kiss on his temple and another on his cheek.

"Hi, Mom," he said without looking up, accepting the kisses like a breeze through the open window.

Barry, Ryan, Bill, and me at a park near our house in December 2008.

Epilogue

By Ryan Tompkins

When I look at the photos of me in the hospital, it's hard for me to believe that I ever looked like that. But it doesn't scare me. I'm not sure why, but it doesn't. I know it's me in that bed, but it just doesn't seem like it's me. I don't remember any of it. I think I remember little bits and pieces from Kentfield Rehab. Basically I don't remember anything until I got home.

When I got home from the hospital, aside from having a hard time getting around, I had a lot of memory trouble. It's finally now just getting better. I write everything down on sticky notes and post them on my computer, but I still forget to write stuff down sometimes. When I went back to school, I could not remember my daily schedule, so I followed a friend of mine who had the same schedule as I did. I realize that I may take more time to do the same work as my friends, but I try hard and I usually get it done.

I also suffered two seizures in the year after the accident, so I couldn't get my driver's license until 2008, when I was eighteen. Unfortunately, three weeks later, I got into an accident and totaled my parents' car. Then a few weeks after that, I had a grand mal seizure because one of the doctors had decided it was okay to take me off one of my seizure medications. Now I have to wait another year or so before I can apply for a license again.

The other big event of 2008 was meeting my birth family. I always wanted to meet them, but I knew I had to wait until I was eighteen. My mom contacted them in Hawaii a couple months before my eighteenth birthday. I found out that Tony and Seyth got married eight years after I was born and had another son eleven years after I was born. Then they had a daughter. I was so happy to find out that I had a seven-year-old brother and a five-year-old sister—and two grandmothers and tons of aunts and uncles and cousins. My parents and I flew over to Oahu and spent a week with them. Tony and Seyth had a big party at their house in Kailua one night so that I could meet everyone. I feel really lucky to have two families that love me so much.

The third major event was getting accepted into college. I'll be going to Mitchell College in New London, Connecticut.

Even though I don't remember the accident or the hospitals, you don't go through something like that without it changing you in some way. After my accident, I learned not to be afraid to take risks, which doesn't mean I take big risks still. It just means I have gained confidence in my ability to make good decisions before I do something risky. Before my accident, I would skateboard down a steep hill without knowing whether I could do it without falling. Now I can look at a hill and know whether it is safe for me to go down it. Because of this, I ride with more confidence. Now I know my limits, and I always wear my helmet.

I have also learned to live life more fully. I don't want to waste one second of what I've been given. Before the accident, I used to watch more TV. Now I feel like I've wasted a day if I watch too much. I prefer to go out to the garage and build something with my hands. I have a lot of tools. I even collect old ones, and I feel more satisfied when I work with them instead of sitting in front of the tube.

Finally, I learned how much I am loved. So many people came to see me in the hospital. They brought gifts and dinners for my parents and so many good wishes for my recovery. I came to realize how many friends I really have. I have a book that everybody signed when they came to visit me in the hospital. I like to look at it because it reminds me of how many people care. Before I didn't know that everyone I knew cared about me. I don't remember anybody coming to visit me, and that's why I'm so glad I have this book to remind me.

I think that my accident changed my mom more than it changed me. First I have to say she was a good mom before the accident. I remember all the great road trips to Lake Tahoe. We always make each other laugh about really stupid things. She makes the best cornbread and always made me the best birthday cakes and always baked poppy seed muffins on Christmas morning. But there were also times when she was too hard on me and made me feel bad about myself. But since the accident, she doesn't get mad as easily and is a lot more compassionate about my feelings. She now lets me do things my way, however strange my way is, more often than not. I've always loved my mom even when she was a little crusty and annoying. I have a great mom, and, of course, she is very lucky to have me as a son, even if I am a pain in the butt (ha-ha).

Afterword

February 2009

It has been two and a half years since Ryan returned home from Kentfield Rehab. He is finishing his last semester of high school and has been accepted to Mitchell College in New London, Connecticut. In the summer of 2008, after he turned eighteen, he met many branches of his birth family in Hawaii and, with a feast at his birth parents' home in Oahu, was feted like a favorite son.

Barry and I look at Ryan and see a tall, good-looking, happy young man. He listens to his iPod and spends too much time on Facebook and watches reruns of *House* and eats pizza on Friday night and balks at doing his British Literature homework and hurls his 250-pound, six-foot-four-inch body onto our bed when we're slow to get up.

Normal. Fun. Great.

So we forget. And we're blindsided again.

We shouldn't be, I know. We know his brain isn't the same as it once was. But he is such a great kid most of the time that we lull ourselves into thinking he is healed.

Then he kicks a hole in the kitchen wall. Or explodes in a profanity-laced tirade at a school administrator. Or bucks and lurches in bed from a grand mal seizure. Or buries an ax in our Japanese maple tree. Or thrusts his fist through a mirror. Or after rattling his brain in a car accident in December 2008, he rips the newspaper from my hands and lights it on fire.

Brain injuries are the wounds that keep on wounding.

I wish I could say that Ryan, Barry, and I have met each challenge with grace and pluck, that we are riding high on a movie-of-the-week appreciation of each other and of life itself. Perhaps we handle things better than most. Heaven knows we've had practice. But in the past two years, along with the celebrations, we have had dark moments, the howling-in-the-bathroom, I've-got-nothing-left moments. Then everything's fine again. Ryan is calm and funny and loving. The best kid in the world. He doesn't drink or do drugs. He doesn't smoke. He still likes hanging out with us. He's friendly and well-mannered. Barry and I remind ourselves how lucky we are.

Then something else happens.

It is the relentlessness, and unpredictability, of brain injuries that wear you out. You're always worried. You're always scared that something truly awful will happen. Will he hurt someone during an emotional outburst? Will he hurt himself? Will he make such a huge error in judgment that he lands in jail?

You think about these things. And you look for help. What should we be doing that we haven't already done? How can we keep our son safe?

Here is what we have learned about brain injuries and the health-care system: Once you're released from acute-care rehabilitation, and once you no longer qualify for outpatient speech therapy, occupational therapy, and physical therapy, you are more or less on your own. No single doctor is in charge. The neurosurgeon's work is long past finished. The neurologist isn't a brain-injury expert or rehab expert, and, at least in our case, has provided little practical guidance. The neuro-psychiatrist only does testing; other people are supposed to apply the results to actual therapy. We have yet to find those people. They apparently all work in rehab facilities and provide therapy only to patients living there. Ryan's psychiatrist prescribes meds to treat current symptoms—impulsivity, seizures, mood swings, inattention—but is not equipped to put together an overall treatment plan. The rehab doctor's responsibility ends when you leave rehab.

So it's left to Barry and me to figure out what to do, though we've been lucky in that Ryan's rehab doctor, Deborah Doherty, is always willing to help us out, when no other medical professional has any answers. But she is crazy-busy, so we are careful not to abuse her generosity.

Mostly we read everything we can. We watch Ryan closely. Why is he so emotionally unstable? Why is he gaining weight? Why is he so tired? Has the shunt stopped working? Is there a new bleed? Does he need more medication? Less medication? Different medication?

We had Ryan in talk therapy for almost a year to work on his anger issues, but it made no discernible difference. We had him in a teen program at a meditation center called Spirit Rock every Sunday for more than a year, then added Tuesday nights with a meditation teacher/psychotherapist. Maybe these sessions had an impact. We can't tell.

The only treatment that has made an observable difference is medication. He is taking valproic acid (Depakote), Neurontin, and Abilify. He is also on Adderall for his now-amplified ADHD. In the fall of 2008, after a series of tests, our neurologist determined Ryan no longer needed to be on valproic acid, a front-line antiseizure med. A month later, Ryan suffered a grand mal seizure. So he is back on the valproic acid.

The medication dulls him somewhat, and he is sleepy by late afternoon, interfering with his ability to study. He has also gained weight, a common side effect of his various meds. But decreasing or eliminating medications puts him at too high a risk not only of life-threatening seizures but of dangerous behavior. I have learned to ignore those who are appalled at the number of pills my son takes every day. They have no clue what he and we have been through or what's at stake for Ryan and us.

We keep in touch with other parents and patients we met at Kentfield Rehab, and their frustrations mirror our own. Everyone is doing amazingly well, considering the devastating injuries they sustained, but as time goes by, the ups and downs take a toll. All the parents we talk with feel there is something more they should be doing, some treatment or specialist they have missed.

When we left Kentfield, Niki—the Chico State student severely injured in a boating accident—couldn't speak or seem to understand what was said to her. Now she is a marvel. She has had twelve surgeries to rebuild her skull and face. She has a prosthetic eye. She looks beautiful. And despite the devastating damage to the speech center in her brain, not only has she learned to speak again, she is a chatterbox. She often has a difficult time, though, retrieving the words she wants to use, a condition called Broca's Aphasia. She had been one class short of earning her bachelor's degree from Chico State, and in December 2008 she finished the class—with lots of accommodations—and got her diploma. She is working one day a week in her parents' dental office and volunteering as a teacher's aide at a local elementary school. She has been seeing a counselor to deal with the anger she feels toward the driver of the boat that caused her injury.

"All in all, she is doing better than anyone could have expected," Niki's mother, Cindy, says.

Brett's progress has been less dramatic. He was Ryan's wonderful roommate at Kentfield, the one whose sister found him on the kitchen floor, unconscious. After three months at Kentfield, Brett spent four months at Casa Colina Transitional Living Center. He struggled to walk because of the persistent stroke-like symptoms on his left side. He had shoulder surgery then foot surgery. He returned to his parents' home in Napa, where he continued physical therapy and attended weekly group sessions with a neuropsychiatrist. But at thirty years old, he hated being dependent on his parents. So after four months, in August 2008, he moved to another transitional living center. Now he's living in a group home in Santa Rosa, about forty minutes from his parents. He's taking a coping-skills class at the local community college and is back in group therapy with the neuropsychiatrist. He still has trouble with his left arm and leg. His memory is poor. He can't drive.

But, like Ryan and Niki, Brett is a survivor. All three have some anger and frustration, but they're fundamentally happy, loving people. As parents we continually remind ourselves—and each other—how far they have come and how lucky we are.

Owen, Ryan's first roommate at Kentfield, still struggles with right-side weakness. His right hand is essentially useless from nerve damage. He has had several surgeries, including one that used bone from his hip to reconstruct his damaged jaw. He has had so much trouble eating that he qualified to receive medical marijuana to boost his appetite. The marijuana, his mother, Wendy, says, has also helped blunt his anger and argumentativeness. Owen, who turned twenty-one in November 2008, recently married and has a one-year-old daughter. Another baby is on the way. He and his wife live with her mother and grandparents.

Josh, who was in a semivegetative state when we last saw him at Kentfield, now is speaking in full sentences and reading. He's walking with a walker and beginning to learn to walk on his own. His right hand doesn't work and his left has Parkinson's-like tremors. He began attending his local community college in September 2007. He currently is taking a typing class, adaptive physical education, speech, and swimming. He's living at home with his mother, Darlene.

Scott was released from prison in March 2009 after serving two and a half years. He is living in a studio apartment near his parents. He works at a local grocery store and attends College of Marin.

We are happy, of course, that Ryan plans to attend college in September 2009. He wants to major in business so he can open his own car restoration garage someday. But we're worried that he will forget to take his medications or he will fail to get enough sleep and, as a consequence, suffer seizures or explosions. We're afraid that his impulsivity and poor judgment—which were issues before the accident and now are amplified—will get him in trouble. We worry, worry, worry. Barry and I plan to rent an apartment in New London so we can be nearby at least for the first semester.

How do we figure out the right thing to do?

We can't. We make the smartest decisions we can each day based on the best information we have.

What we can do is love him and love him and love him.

For all we have been through, there is so little I know for certain except for maybe this: Motherhood is about raising—and celebrating—the child you have, not the child you thought you would have. It's about understanding that he is exactly the person he is supposed to be. And that, if you're lucky, he just might be the teacher who turns you into the person you are supposed to be.

Acknowledgments

I sometimes get wistful for the days I spent in the Marin General and UC–San Francisco waiting rooms. For as awful as they were, I miss the daily, sometimes hourly, reminders that my family and I are completely loved. It has occurred to me that I wrote this book simply to have a public forum in which to thank all the friends and family who made us food and made us laugh, who hugged us and dragged us out for walks and cried at all the right times and who—most important of all—believed in Ryan as fiercely as we did.

Barry's daughter Andi flew up from Los Angeles with her sons, Kyle and Jared, and helped us ask the right questions and keep level heads and—this is one reason we are such good friends—she distracted me with great celebrity gossip. Barry's younger daughter, Lainie, flew in from Washington, D.C., to make sure we laughed.

My parents, Bob and Peg Ryan, did what they have done all my life: made me feel safe and loved. Whatever strength I have comes from them; whatever failings as a parent are my own. The greatest tribute to parents, I think, is that their grown children would choose them as friends. We would, and we have, as evidenced by my brothers' and sisters' presence every weekend for dinner and drinks on my parents' back patio.

My sisters, Barbara and Donna, and my brothers, Ken and Gerard, are always my first line of defense in a crisis. Despite being three thousand miles away in Florida, they still were like the Jets in *West Side Story*, snapping their fingers behind me, battling the enemy in Ryan's head with prayer and will, reminding me that we had plenty of muscle on our side. Ken sent Ryan a special plaque that depicted a bas relief of two boxers over the words: "Ryan Tompkins: HALL OF FAME. For fighting a hard battle. Keep answering every bell and never give up the fight."

Barry and I owe so much to the dozens and dozens of friends, neighbors, teachers, shopkeepers, and colleagues who poured into the hospitals to sit with us or brought lovely meals to our home or said prayers. Tia O'Brien and Judi Shils made sure Bill the dog was walked and fed. My friends at the *San Francisco Chronicle* complied with the one stipulation I made for their visits: to arrive with at least one good piece of gossip. A complete list of people who deserve thanks is impossible. I think we received visits, cards, or phone calls from just about every resident in our little town of Ross. All of you are in my heart forever.

But I do have to single out several people. They are my clan, my tribe, my group of friends who are connected to Barry, Ryan, and me not by blood but by love and loyalty. Barry and I owe more than we can ever repay to: Doug Smith and Ben and Emma Stevens-Smith, Erin and Rob Becker, Jill and Steve Kantola, Devyani Kamdar, Jeanne Barr, Jan and Greg McAdoo, Mickey and Norma Freeman, Chris and Eric Lindner, Suzanne, Jeff, and Josh Appleman, Sharon and Gary Gustafson, and Yvonne and Todd Middleton.

Lorna Stevens gets her own paragraph. One editor who read a draft of the book suggested there was too much of Lorna on the pages. "There isn't enough," I told him. "The book does no justice to how much she really did." If I had a wish for my son, it would be that he has a friend in his life like Lorna. She protected me and uplifted me. She allowed me to focus completely on Ryan. She gave me room to rediscover myself as a mother. She also read several versions of the book, filling gaps in my memory and providing the cheerleading I needed to write the next draft. I thank Doug, Ben, and Emma for sharing her with me.

Thank you to Andi, Lainie, Erin, and Jan who read various drafts and pushed me to keep asking myself how I felt, what I thought, how I changed. Erin and Rob gave me four quiet days at their West Marin ranch to plow through a difficult rewrite. I thank Ken Conner, Yvonne Middleton, Chris Lindner, and Roy Eisenhardt, too, for their careful reading of the manuscript and thoughtful feedback. Thanks, also, to David Lewis, who taught me the difference between reporting stories and telling them.

Thank you to Dr. Mark Eastham, who fact-checked the medical parts of the book and tracked down CT scans for me. So many wonderful professionals helped save Ryan's life and guide Barry and me through this complicated and wrenching ordeal but in particular Dr. Eastham and nurse Jimette Rosas of Marin General, Dr. Nalin Gupta—who also read a draft and helped me make corrections—and Dr. Scott Soifer and Dr. Jeff Fineman of UCSF, and Dr. Geoff Manley of San Francisco General, and to Larry and Pam Baer for sending Dr. Manley to us. Dr. Deborah Doherty of Kentfield Rehabilitation and Specialty Hospital has continued to be our go-to person in a crisis. She called us from vacation when Ryan suffered a seizure at Lake Tahoe during the Christmas holidays in 2008. She has been incredibly forthright and caring— qualities that separate the good doctors from the great ones. Dr. Doherty and all of the doctors mentioned were kind enough to sit for interviews and help me translate Ryan's medical records into English.

I thank Dr. Bill Gonda for his steady counsel and comforting presence and Dr. Brian Salmen, Dr. Toni Brayer, and Dr. Elizabeth Robbins for their timely and important help.

At Kentfield Rehab, we are particularly grateful to case-worker Debbie Baniadam and aide Clemania Felix, both of whom watched over Ryan as if he were their own child. And to our fellow travelers on this difficult road—Owen, Brett, Niki, Josh, and their lovely families—I continue to be inspired by all of you.

I am grateful to my agent, Betsy Lerner, who waited twelve years between books, and to my editor, Sydny Miner at Simon & Schuster, for shepherding this project from beginning to end.

For more than a year, I have tied up tables at Coffee Roasters in San Anselmo and Taste of Rome (formerly Café Trieste) in Sausalito. These establishments let me tap away on my laptop as long as I liked, supplying my two basic needs: caffeine and free wi-fi.

Thanks to Ryan for allowing me to splay his life across the pages of this book.

Last, I thank Barry—for his strength (I'd go into any battle anywhere with this man), for encouraging me to tell our story honestly and for having the patience to wait for me to learn what he has always known: How to love people for who they are, without fear or reservation.